ROOKIE COACHES BASKETBALL GUIDE

American Coaching Effectiveness Program

Leisure Press
Champaign, Illinois

Library of Congress Cataloging-in-Publication Data

Rookie coaches basketball guide / by American Coaching Effectiveness
  Program.
      p. cm.
    ISBN 0-88011-412-6
    1. Basketball--Coaching.   I. American Coaching Effectiveness
Program.
  GV885.3.R66   1991
  796.323'07'7--dc20   90-40062
                                                            CIP
ISBN: 0-88011-412-6

Basketball Consultant and
  Developmental Editor: Ted Miller
Production Editor: Julia Anderson
Copyeditor: Wendy Nelson
Proofreader: Linda Siegel
Production Director: Ernie Noa
Typesetters: Angela K. Snyder, Brad Colson
Text Design: Keith Blomberg
Text Layout: Kimberlie Henris
Cover Design: Jack Davis
Cover Photo: John Kilroy
Illustrations: Keith Blomberg, Tim Stiles, Gretchen Walters
Printer: United Graphics

Leisure Press books are available at special discounts for bulk purchase for sales promotions, premiums, fund-raising, or educational use. Special editions or book excerpts can also be created to specification. For details, contact the Special Sales Manager at Leisure Press.

Printed in the United States of America

10 9 8 7 6 5 4 3

Leisure Press   *Europe Office:*
A Division of Human Kinetics Publishers, Inc.   Human Kinetics Publishers (Europe) Ltd.
Box 5076, Champaign, IL 61825-5076   P.O. Box IW14
1-800-747-4457   Leeds LS16 6TR
                                                     England
Canada Office: 0532-781708
P.O. Box 2503, Windsor, ON N8Y 4S2
1-800-465-7301 (in Canada only)   *Australia Office:*
                                                     Human Kinetics Publishers
                                                     P.O. Box 80
                                                     Kingswood 5062
                                                     South Australia
                                                     374-0433

Contents

Welcome to Coaching!

Coaching young people is an exciting way to be involved in sport. But it isn't easy. Some coaches are overwhelmed by the responsibilities involved in helping athletes through their early sport experiences. And that's not surprising, because coaching youngsters requires more than rolling out the balls and letting them play. It involves preparing them physically and mentally to compete effectively, fairly, and safely in their sport and providing them a positive role model.

This book will help you meet the challenges *and* experience the many rewards of coaching young athletes. We call it the *Rookie Coaches Basketball Guide* because it is intended for adults with little or no formal preparation in coaching basketball. In this *Rookie Guide* you'll learn how to apply general coaching principles and teach basketball rules, skills, and strategies successfully to kids.

This book also serves as a text for the American Coaching Effectiveness Program's (ACEP) Rookie Coaches Course. If you would like more information about the Rookie Coaches Course or any of the other courses ACEP offers, please contact us at:

ACEP
Box 5076
Champaign, IL 61825-5076
1-800-747-5698

Good coaching!

UNIT 1

Who Me . . . a Coach?

If you're like most youth league coaches, you were recruited from the ranks of concerned parents, sport enthusiasts, or community volunteers. And, like many rookie *and* veteran coaches, you probably have had little formal instruction on how to coach. But when the call went out for coaches to assist with the local youth basketball program, you answered because you like children, enjoy basketball, are community-minded, and perhaps are interested in starting a coaching career.

I Want to Help, But . . .

Your initial coaching assignment may be difficult. Like many volunteers, you may not know everything there is to know about basketball, nor about how to work with children between the ages of 6 and 14. Relax, this *Rookie Coaches Basketball Guide* will help you learn the basics for coaching basketball effectively. In the coming pages you will find the answers to such common questions as the following:

- What tools do I need to be a good coach?
- How can I best communicate with my players?
- How do I go about teaching sport skills?
- What can I do to promote safety?
- What actions do I take when someone is injured?
- What are the basic rules, skills, and strategies of basketball?
- What practice drills will improve my players' basketball skills?

1

Before answering these questions, let's take a look at what's involved in being a coach.

Am I a Parent or a Coach?

Many coaches are parents, but the two roles should not be confused. As a parent you are responsible only to yourself and your child; as a coach you are responsible to the organization, all the players on the team (including your child), their parents, and yourself. When

you assume these additional responsibilities as a coach, your son or daughter may not understand why you behave differently on the basketball court than you do at home. To avoid problems, take the following steps when coaching your child:

- Ask your child if he or she wants you to coach the team.
- Explain why you wish to be involved with the team.
- Discuss with your child your new responsibilities and how they will affect your relationship when coaching.
- Limit your "coach" behavior to those times when you are in a coaching role.
- Avoid parenting during practice or game

situations to keep your role clear in your child's mind.
- Reaffirm your love for your child irrespective of his or her performance on the basketball court.

What Are My Responsibilities as a Coach?

A coach assumes the responsibility of doing everything possible to ensure that the youngsters on his or her team will have an enjoyable and safe sporting experience while they learn sport skills. If you're ever in doubt about your approach, remind yourself that "fun and fundamentals" are most important.

Provide an Enjoyable Experience

Sport should be fun. Even if nothing else is accomplished, make certain your players have fun. Take the fun out of sport and you'll take the kids out of sport.

Children enter sport for a number of reasons (e.g., to meet and play with other children, to develop physically, to learn skills), but their major objective is to have fun. Help them satisfy this goal by injecting humor and variety into your practices. Also, make games nonthreatening, festive experiences for your players. Such an approach will increase their desire for future participation, which should be the primary goal of youth sport. Unit 2 will help you learn how to satisfy your players' yearning for fun and keep winning in perspective. And, unit 3 will describe how to communicate this perspective effectively to them.

Provide a Safe Experience

You are responsible for planning and teaching activities in such a way that the progression between activities minimizes risks (see units 4 and 5). You also must ensure that the facility at which your team practices and plays, and the equipment team members use, are free of hazards. Finally, you need to protect yourself from any legal liability issues that might arise from your involvement as a coach. Unit 5 will help you take the appropriate precautions.

Teach Basic Basketball Skills

In becoming a coach, you take on the role of educator. You must teach your players the fundamental skills and strategies necessary for success in basketball. That means that you need to "go to school." You'll also find that you are better able to teach the basketball skills and strategies you do know if you plan your practices. Unit 4 of this manual provides guidelines for effective practice planning.

If you don't know the basics of basketball now, you can learn them by reading the second half of this manual. And even if you know basketball as a player, do you know how to teach it? This book will help you get started. Furthermore, many valuable basketball books are available, including those offered by Human Kinetics Publishers. See the order form in the back of this book or call 1-800-747-4457 for more information.

Who Can Help?

Veteran coaches in your league are an especially good source of information and assistance. You can also learn a great deal by observing local high school coaches in practices and games. You might even ask a few of the coaches you respect most to lend a hand with a couple of your practices. These coaches have experienced the same emotions and concerns you are facing; their advice and feedback can be invaluable as you work through your first seasons of coaching. You can get additional help by attending basketball clinics, reading basketball publications, and studying instructional videos. Finally, the American Coaching Effectiveness Program, the local organization for which you coach, and the following national organizations will assist you in obtaining more basketball coaching information.

National Association of Basketball Coaches
P.O. Box 307
Branford, CT 06405
(203) 488-1232

USA Basketball
1750 East Boulder Street
Colorado Springs, CO 80909
(719) 632-3227

Women's Basketball Coaches Association
4646 B Lawrenceville Highway
Lilburn, Georgia 30247
Telephone (404) 279-8027
Facsimile (404) 279-8473

Coaching basketball is a rewarding experience. And, just as you want your players to learn and practice to be the best they can be, learn all you can about coaching so you can be the best basketball coach you can be.

UNIT 2

What Tools Do I Need to Coach?

Have you purchased the traditional coaching tools—things like whistles, coaching clothes, basketball shoes, and a clipboard? They'll help you coach, but to be a successful coach you'll need five other *tools* that cannot be bought. These tools are available only through self-examination and hard work, but they're easy to remember with the acronym COACH:

C—Comprehension
O—Outlook
A—Affection
C—Character
H—Humor

Comprehension

Comprehension of the rules, skills, and tactics of basketball is required. It is essential that you understand the basic elements of the sport. To assist you in learning about the game, the second half of this guide describes the rules, skills, and tactics of basketball, and suggests how to plan for the season and individual practices. In the basketball-specific section of this guide, you'll also find a variety of drills to use in developing young players' basketball skills.

To improve your comprehension of basketball, take the following steps:

- Read the sport-specific section of this book.
- Consider reading other basketball coaching books, including those available from ACEP (see p. 74 to order).
- Contact any of the organizations listed on page 3.
- Attend basketball coaches' clinics.
- Talk with other, more experienced basketball coaches.
- Observe local college, high school, and youth basketball games.
- Watch basketball games on television.

In addition to having basketball knowledge, you must implement proper training and safety methods so your players can participate with little risk of injury. Even then, sport injuries will occur. And, more often than not, you'll be the first person responding to your players' injuries. Therefore, make sure you understand the basic emergency care procedures described in unit 5. Also read in that unit how to handle more serious sport injury situations.

Outlook

This coaching tool refers to your perspective and goals—what you are seeking as a coach. The most common coaching objectives are: (a) to have fun, (b) to help players develop their physical, mental, and social skills, and (c) to win. Thus *outlook* involves the priorities you set, your planning, and your vision for the future.

To work successfully with children in a sport setting, you must have your priorities in order. In just what order do you rank the importance of fun, development, and winning?

Answer the following questions to examine your objectives.

Of which situation would you be most proud?

a. Knowing that each participant enjoyed playing basketball.
b. Seeing that all players improved their basketball skills.
c. Winning the league championship.

Which statement best reflects your thoughts about sport?

a. If it isn't fun, don't do it.
b. Everyone should learn something every day.
c. Sport isn't fun if you don't win.

How would you like your players to remember you?

a. As a coach who was fun to play for.
b. As a coach who provided a good base of fundamental skills.
c. As a coach who had a winning record.

Which would you most like to hear a parent of a child on your team say?

a. Billy really had a good time playing basketball this year.
b. Susie learned some important lessons playing basketball this year.
c. Ronnie played on the first place basketball team this year.

Which of the following would be the most rewarding moment of your season?

a. Having your team not want to stop playing even after practice is over.
b. Observing your players finally master the skill of dribbling without looking at the ball.
c. Winning the league championship.

Look over your answers. If you most often selected "a" responses, then having fun is more important to you. A majority of "b" answers suggests that skill development is what attracts you to coaching. And if "c" was your most frequent response, winning is tops on your list of coaching priorities.

Most coaches say fun and development are more important, but when actually coaching, some coaches emphasize—indeed overemphasize—winning. You too will face situations that challenge you to keep winning in its proper perspective. During such moments you'll have to choose between emphasizing your players' development or winning. If your priorities are in order, your players' well-being will take precedence over your team's win-loss record every time.

Take the following actions to better define your outlook:

- Determine your priorities for the season.
- Prepare for situations that challenge your priorities.
- Set goals for yourself and your players that are consistent with those priorities.
- Plan how you and your players can best attain those goals.
- Review your goals frequently to be sure that you are staying on track.

It is particularly important for coaches to permit all young athletes to participate. Each youngster should have an opportunity to develop skills and have fun—even if it means sacrificing a win or two during the season. After all, wouldn't you prefer losing a couple of games to losing a couple of players' interest in sport?

Remember that the challenge and joy of sport is experienced through *striving to win*, not through winning itself. Players who aren't allowed off the bench are denied the opportunity to strive to win. And herein lies the irony: A coach who allows all of his or her players to participate and develop skills will, in the end, come out on top.

ACEP has a motto that will help you keep your outlook in the best interest of the kids on your team. It summarizes in four words all you need to remember when establishing your coaching priorities:

Athletes First, Winning Second

This motto recognizes that striving to win is an important, even vital part of sport. But it emphatically states that no efforts in striving to win should be made at the expense of athletes' well-being, development, and enjoyment.

Affection

This is another vital *tool* you will want to have in your coaching kit: a genuine concern for the young people you coach. *Affection* involves having a love for children, a desire to share with them your love and knowledge of sport, and the patience and understanding that allows each individual playing for you to grow from his or her involvement in basketball.

Successful coaches have a real concern for the health and welfare of their players. They care that each child on the team has an enjoyable and successful experience. They have a strong desire to work with children and be involved in their growth. And they have the patience to work with those who are slower to learn or less capable of performing. If you have such qualities or are willing to work hard to develop them, then you have the affection necessary to coach young athletes.

There are many ways to demonstrate your affection and patience, including the following:

- Make an effort to get to know each player on your team.
- Treat each player as an individual.
- Empathize with players' trying to learn new and difficult basketball skills.
- Treat players as you would like to be treated under similar circumstances.
- Be in control of your emotions.
- Show your enthusiasm for being involved with your team.
- Keep an upbeat and positive tone in all of your communications.

Character

Youngsters learn by listening to what adults say. But they learn even more by watching the behaviors of certain important individuals. As a coach, you are likely to be a significant figure in the lives of your players. Will you be a good role model?

Having good *character* means modeling appropriate behaviors for sport and life. That means more than just saying the right things. What you say and what you do must match. There is no place in coaching for the "Do as I say, not as I do" philosophy. Be in control before, during, and after all games and practices. And don't be afraid to admit that you were wrong. No one is perfect!

Consider the following steps to being a good role model:

- Take stock of your strengths and weaknesses.
- Build on your strengths.
- Set goals for yourself to improve upon those areas you would not like to see mimicked.
- If you slip up, apologize to your team and to yourself. You'll do better next time.

Humor

Humor is often overlooked as a coaching tool. For our use it means having the ability to laugh *at* yourself and *with* your players during practices and games. Nothing helps balance the tone of a serious, skill-learning session like a chuckle or two. And a sense of humor puts in perspective the many mistakes your young players will make. So don't get upset over each miscue or respond negatively to erring players. Allow your players and yourself to enjoy the "ups" and don't dwell on the "downs."

Here are some tips for injecting humor into your practices:

- Make practices fun by including a variety of activities.
- Keep all players involved in drills and scrimmages.
- Consider laughter by your players a sign of enjoyment, not a lack of discipline.
- Smile!

Where Do You Stand?

To take stock of your "coaching tool kit," rank yourself on each of the three questions concerning the five coaching tools. Simply circle the number that best describes your *present* status on each item.

Not at all		Somewhat		Very much so
1	2	3	4	5

Comprehension

1. Could you explain the rules of basketball to other parents without studying for a long time?   1 2 3 4 5
2. Do you know how to organize and conduct safe basketball practices?   1 2 3 4 5
3. Do you know how to provide first aid for most common, minor sport injuries?   1 2 3 4 5

Comprehension Score: _____

Outlook

4. Do you have winning in its proper perspective when you coach?   1 2 3 4 5
5. Do you plan for every meeting and practice?   1 2 3 4 5
6. Do you have a vision of what you want your players to be able to do by the end of the season?   1 2 3 4 5

Outlook Score: _____

Affection

7. Do you enjoy working with children?   1 2 3 4 5
8. Are you patient with youngsters learning new skills?   1 2 3 4 5
9. Are you able to show your players that you care?   1 2 3 4 5

Affection Score: _____

Character

10. Are your words and behaviors consistent with each other?   1 2 3 4 5
11. Are you a good model for your players?   1 2 3 4 5
12. Do you keep negative emotions under control before, during, and after games?   1 2 3 4 5

Character Score: _____

Humor

13. Do you usually smile at your players?   1 2 3 4 5
14. Are your practices fun?   1 2 3 4 5
15. Are you able to laugh at your mistakes?   1 2 3 4 5

Humor Score: _____

If you scored 9 or less on any of the coaching tools, be sure to reread those sections carefully. And even if you scored 15 on each tool, don't be complacent. Keep learning! Then you'll be well-equipped with the tools you need to coach young athletes.

UNIT 3

How Should I Communicate With My Players?

EVERYBODY GOT THAT?

Now you know the tools needed to COACH: Comprehension, Outlook, Affection, Character, and Humor are essential for effective coaching. Without them, you'd have a difficult time getting started. But none of these tools will work if you don't know how to use them with your athletes—that requires skillful communication. This unit examines what communication is and how you can become a more effective communicator-coach.

What's Involved in Communication?

Coaches often believe that communication involves only instructing players to do something, but these verbal commands are a very small part of the communication process. More than half of what is communicated in a message is nonverbal. So remember when you are coaching, "actions speak louder than words."

Communication in its simplest form involves two people: a *sender* and a *receiver*. The sender can transmit the message verbally, through facial expression, and via body language. Once the message is sent, the receiver must try to determine the meaning of the message. A receiver who fails to attend or listen will miss part, if not all, of the message.

How Can I Send More Effective Messages?

Young athletes often have little understanding of the rules and skills of basketball, and probably even have less confidence in playing it. So they need accurate, understandable, and supportive messages to help them along. That's why it's so important for you to send verbal and nonverbal messages effectively.

Verbal Messages

"Sticks and stones may break my bones, but words will never hurt me," isn't true. Spoken words can have a strong and long-lasting effect. And coaches' words are particularly influential, because youngsters place great importance on what coaches say. Therefore, whether you are correcting a misbehavior, teaching a player how to dribble the ball, or praising a player for good effort,

- *be positive, but honest;*
- *state it clearly and simply;*
- *say it loud enough and say it again; and*
- *be consistent.*

Be Positive, But Honest

Nothing turns people off like hearing someone nag all the time. Young athletes are similarly discouraged by a coach who gripes constantly. The kids on your team need encouragement because many of them doubt their ability to play basketball. So *look* for and *tell* your players what they did well.

On the other hand, don't cover up poor or incorrect play with rosy words of praise. Kids know all too well when they've made a mistake, and no cheerfully expressed cliché can undo their errors. And, if you fail to acknowl-

edge players' errors your athletes will think you are a phony.

A good way to handle situations in which you have identified and must correct improper technique is to serve your players a "compliment sandwich."

1. Point out what the athlete did correctly.
2. Let the player know what was incorrect in the performance and instruct him or her how to correct it.
3. Encourage the player by reemphasizing what he or she did well.

State It Clearly and Simply

Positive and honest messages are good, but only if expressed directly and in words your players understand. "Beating around the bush" is an ineffective and inefficient way to send messages verbally. If you ramble, your players will miss the point of your message and probably lose interest. Below are some tips for saying things clearly.

- Organize your thoughts before speaking to your athletes.
- Explain things thoroughly, but don't bore them with long-winded monologues.
- Use language that your players can understand. However, avoid trying to be "hip" by using their age group's slang words.

Say It Loud Enough and Say It Again

A crowded gym filled with the sound of bouncing balls can hinder communication. So talk to your team in a voice that all members can hear and interpret. It's okay, in fact appropriate, to soften your voice when speaking to a player individually about a personal problem. But most of the time your messages will be for all your players to hear; so make sure they can! A word of caution, however: Don't dominate the setting with a booming voice that detracts attention from players' performances.

Sometimes what you say, even if stated loud and clear, won't sink in the first time. This may be particularly true with young athletes hearing words they don't understand. To avoid boring repetition but still get your message across, say the same thing in a slightly different way. For instance, you might first tell your players, "Put defensive pressure on your opponent." Then, soon thereafter, remind them "Play your opponent tight; cut-off the dribble, get in the passing lanes, and prevent easy shots." The second message may get through to some players who missed it the first time around.

Be Consistent

People often say things in a way that implies a different message. For example, a touch of sarcasm added to the words "way to go" sends an entirely different message than the words themselves suggest. It is essential that you avoid sending such mixed messages. Keep the tone of your voice consistent with the words you use. And don't say something one day and contradict it the next; players will get confused.

Nonverbal Messages

Just as you should be consistent in the tone of voice and words you use, you should also keep your verbal and nonverbal messages consistent. An extreme example of failing to do this would be shaking your head, indicating disapproval, while at the same time telling a player "nice try." Which is the player to believe, your gesture or your words?

Messages can be sent nonverbally in a number of ways. Facial expressions and body language are just two of the more obvious forms of nonverbal signals that can help you when you coach.

Facial Expressions

The look on a person's face is the quickest clue to what he or she thinks or feels. Your players know this, so they will study your face, looking for any sign that will tell them more than the words you say. Don't try to fool them by putting on a happy or blank "mask." They'll see through it, and you'll lose credibility.

Serious, stone-faced expressions are no help to kids who need cues as to how they are performing. They will just assume you're unhappy or disinterested. So don't be afraid to smile. A smile from a coach can boost the confidence of an unsure young athlete. Plus, a smile lets your players know that you are happy coaching them. But don't overdo it because your players won't be able to tell when you are genuinely pleased by something they've done or when you are just "putting on" a smiling face.

Body Language

How would your players think you felt if you came to practice slouched over, with head down and shoulders slumped? Tired? Bored? Unhappy? What would they think if you watched them during a contest with your hands on your hips, jaws clenched, and face reddened? Upset with them? Disgusted at an official? Mad at a fan? Probably some or all of these things would enter your players' minds. That's why you should carry yourself in a pleasant, confident, and vigorous manner. Such a posture not only projects happiness with your coaching role, it also provides a good example for young players who may model your behavior.

Physical contact can also be a very important use of body language. A handshake, a pat on the head, an arm around the shoulder, or even a big hug are effective ways of showing approval, concern, affection, or joy to your players. Youngsters are especially in need of this type of nonverbal message. Keep within the obvious moral and legal limits, but don't be reluctant to touch your players and send a message that can only truly be expressed in that way.

How Can I Improve My Receiving Skills?

Now let's examine the other half of the communication process—receiving messages. Too often people are very good senders and very poor receivers of messages; they seem to naturally enjoy hearing themselves talk more than listening to others. As a coach of young athletes it is essential that you receive their verbal and nonverbal messages effectively. You can

be a better receiver of your players' messages if you are willing to read about the keys to receiving messages and then make a strong effort to use them with your players. You'll be surprised what you've been missing.

Attention!

First you must pay attention; you must want to hear what others have to communicate to you. That's not always easy when you're busy coaching and have many things competing for your attention. But in one-to-one or team meetings with players, you must really focus on what they are telling you, both verbally and nonverbally. Not only will such focused attention help you catch every word they say, but you'll also notice their mood and physical state, and you'll get an idea of their feelings toward you and other players on the team.

Listen CARE-FULLY

How we receive messages from others, perhaps more than anything else we do, demonstrates how much we care for the sender and what that person has to tell us. If you care little for your players or have little regard for what they have to say, it will show in how you attend and listen to them. Check yourself. Do you find your mind wandering to what you are going to do after practice while one of your players is talking to you? Do you frequently have to ask your players, "What did you say?" If so, you need to work on your receiving mechanics of attending and listening. If you find that you're missing the messages your players send, perhaps the most critical question you should ask yourself is this: Do I care?

How Do I Put It All Together?

So far we've discussed sending and receiving messages separately. But we all know that senders and receivers switch roles several times during an interaction. One person initiates a communication by sending a message to another person who then receives the message. The receiver then switches roles and becomes the sender by responding to the person who sent the initial message. These verbal and nonverbal responses are called *feedback*.

Your players will be looking to you for feedback all the time. They will want to know how you think they are performing, what you think of their ideas, and whether their efforts please you. *How you respond* will strongly affect your players. So let's take a look at a few general types of feedback and examine their possible effects.

Providing Instructions

With young players, much of your feedback will involve answering questions about how to play the sport. Your instructive responses to these questions should include both verbal and nonverbal feedback. The following are suggestions for giving instructional feedback:

- Keep verbal instructions simple and concise.
- Use demonstrations to provide nonverbal instructional feedback (see unit 4).
- "Walk" players through the skill, or use a slow-motion demonstration if they are having trouble learning.

Correcting Errors

When your players perform incorrectly, you need to provide informative feedback to correct the error—and the sooner the better. And when you do correct errors, keep in mind these two principles: Use negative criticism sparingly, and keep calm.

Use Negative Criticism Sparingly

Although you may need to punish players for horseplay or dangerous activities by scolding or temporarily removing them from activity, avoid reprimanding players for performance errors. Admonishing players for honest mistakes makes them afraid to even try; nothing ruins a youngster's enjoyment of a sport more than a coach who harps on every miscue. So instead, correct your players by using the positive approach. They'll enjoy playing more and you'll enjoy coaching more.

Keep Calm

Don't fly off the handle when your players make mistakes. Remember, you're coaching young and inexperienced players, not pros. You'll therefore see more incorrect than correct technique, and probably have more discipline problems than you expect. But throwing a tantrum over each error or misbehavior will only inhibit them or suggest to them the wrong kind of behavior to model. Let your players know that mistakes aren't the end of the world; and, stay cool!

Positive Feedback

Praising players when they have performed or behaved well is an effective way of getting them to repeat (or try to repeat) that behavior in the future. And positive feedback for effort is an especially effective way to motivate youngsters to work on difficult skills. So rather than shouting and providing negative feedback to a player who has made a mistake, try offering a compliment sandwich, described on page 12.

Sometimes just the way you word feedback can make it more positive than negative. For example, instead of saying, "Don't shoot the ball that way," you might say, "Shoot the ball this way." Then your players will be *focusing on what to do instead of what not to do.*

Coaches, be positive!

Only a very small percentage of ACEP-trained coaches' behaviors are negative.

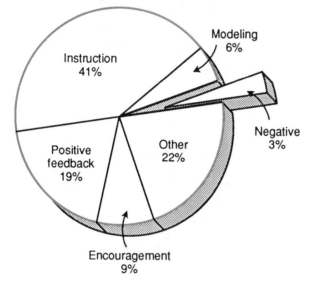

You can give positive feedback verbally and nonverbally. Telling a player, especially in front of teammates, that he or she has performed well, is a great way to increase a kid's confidence. And a pat on the back or a handshake can be a very tangible way of communicating your recognition of a player's performance.

Who Else Do I Need to Communicate With?

Coaching involves not only sending and receiving messages and providing proper feedback to players, but also includes interacting with players' parents, fans, game officials, and opposing coaches. If you don't communicate effectively with these groups of people, your coaching career will be unpleasant, and short-lived. So try these suggestions for communicating with each group.

Parents

A player's parents need to be assured that their son or daughter is under the direction of a coach who is both knowledgeable about basketball and concerned about the youngster's well-being. You can put their worries to rest by holding a preseason parent orientation meeting in which you describe your background and your approach to coaching.

If parents contact you with a concern during the season, listen to them closely and try to offer positive responses. If you need to communicate with parents, catch them after a practice, give them a phone call, or send a note through the mail. Messages sent to parents through children are too often lost, misinterpreted, or forgotten.

Fans

The stands probably won't be overflowing at your games, but that only means that you'll more easily hear the one or two fans who criticize your coaching. When you hear something negative said about the job you're doing, don't respond. Keep calm, consider whether the message had any value, and if not, forget it. The best approach is to put away your "rabbit ears" and communicate to fans through your actions that you are a confident, competent coach.

Even if you are ready to withstand the negative comments of fans, your players may not be. Prepare them. Tell them that it is you, not the spectators, to whom they should listen. If you notice that one of your players is rattled by a fan's comment, reassure the player that your evaluation is more objective and favorable—and the one that counts.

Game Officials

How you communicate with officials will have a great influence on the way your players behave toward them. Therefore, you need to set an example. Greet officials with a handshake, an introduction, and perhaps some casual conversation about the upcoming contest. Indicate your respect for them before, during, and after the contest.

Keep in mind that most youth basketball officials are volunteers. So don't make nasty remarks, shout, or use disrespectful body gestures. Your players will see you do it and they'll get the idea that such behavior is appropriate. Plus, if the official hears or sees you, the communication between the two of you will break down. In short, you take care of the coaching, and let the officials take care of the officiating.

Opposing Coaches

Make an effort to visit with the coach of the opposing team before the game. Perhaps the two of you can work out a special arrangement for the contest, such as matching up players and coordinating substitutions. During the game, don't get into a personal feud with the opposing coach. Remember, it's the kids, not the coaches, who are competing.

Summary Checklist

Now, check your coach-communication skills by answering yes or no to the following questions.

	Yes	No
1. Are your verbal messages to your players positive and honest?	——	——
2. Do you speak loudly, clearly, and in a language your athletes understand?	——	——
3. Do you remember to repeat instructions to your players, in case they didn't hear you the first time?	——	——
4. Are the tone of your voice and your nonverbal messages consistent with the words you use?	——	——
5. Do your facial expressions and body language express interest in and happiness with your coaching role?	——	——
6. Are you attentive to your players and able to pick up even their small verbal and nonverbal cues?	——	——
7. Do you really care about what your athletes say to you?	——	——
8. Do you instruct rather than criticize when your players make errors?	——	——
9. Are you usually positive when responding to things your athletes say and do?	——	——
10. Do you try to communicate in a cooperative and respectful manner with players' parents, fans, game officials, and opposing coaches?	——	——

If you answered "No" to any of the above questions, you may want to refer back to the section of the chapter where the topic was discussed. *Now* is the time to address communication problems, not when you're coaching your players.

How Do I Get My Team Ready to Play?

To coach basketball, you must understand the basic rules, skills, and strategies of the sport. The second part of this *Rookie Coaches Basketball Guide* provides the basic information you'll need to comprehend the sport.

But all the basketball knowledge in the world will do you little good unless you present it effectively to your players. That's why this unit is so important. In it you will learn the steps to take in teaching sport skills, as well as practical guidelines for planning your season and individual practices.

How Do I Teach Sport Skills?

Many people believe that the only qualification needed to coach is to have played the sport. It's helpful to have played, but there is much more to coaching successfully. And even if you haven't played basketball, you can still teach the skills of the game effectively using this IDEA:

I —Introduce the skill.

D—Demonstrate the skill.

E—Explain the skill.

A—Attend to players practicing the skill.

Introduce the Skill

Players, especially young and inexperienced players, need to know what skill they are learning and why they are learning it. You should, therefore, take these three steps every time you introduce a skill to your players:

1. Get your players' attention.
2. Name the skill.
3. Explain the importance of the skill.

Get Your Players' Attention

Because youngsters are easily distracted, use some method to get their attention. Some coaches use interesting news items or stories. Others use jokes. And others simply project an enthusiasm that gets their players to listen. Whatever method you use, speak slightly above the normal volume and look your players in the eye when you speak. Position players so they can see and hear. Arrange them in two or three evenly-spaced rows, facing you and not some source of distraction (a blank wall background is recommended). Then check that all can see and hear you before you begin.

Name the Skill

Although you might mention other common names for the skill, decide which one you'll use and stick with it. This will help avoid confusion and enhance communication among your players. For example, choose either "screen" or "pick" as the term for the appropriate offensive skill, and use it consistently.

Explain the Importance of the Skill

Although the importance of a skill may be apparent to you, your players may be less able to see how the skill will help them become better basketball players. Offer them a reason for learning the skill and describe how the skill relates to more advanced skills.

Demonstrate the Skill

The demonstration step is the most important part of teaching a basketball skill to young players who may have never attempted anything that closely resembles the technique.

They need a picture, not just words. They need to *see* how the skill is performed.

If you are unable to perform the skill correctly, have an assistant coach or someone skilled in basketball perform the demonstration. These tips will help make your demonstrations more effective:

- Use correct form.
- Demonstrate the skill several times.
- Slow down the skill, if possible, during one or two performances so players can see every movement involved in the skill.
- Perform the skill at different angles so your players can get a full perspective of it.
- Demonstrate the skill with both the right and left hand.

Explain the Skill

Players learn more effectively when they're given a brief explanation of the skill along with the demonstration. Use simple terms to describe the skill and, if possible, relate the skill to previously learned skills. Ask your players if they understand your description. If one of them looks confused, have him or her explain the skill back to you.

The most difficult aspect of coaching is this: Coaches must learn to let athletes learn. Sport skills should be taught so they have meaning to the child, not just meaning to the coach.

Rainer Martens, ACEP Founder

Complex skills often are better understood when they are explained in more manageable parts. For instance, if you want to teach your players how to change direction when they dribble the ball, you might take the following steps:

1. Show them a correct performance of the entire skill and explain its function in basketball.
2. Break down the skill and point out its component parts to your players.
3. Have players perform each of the component skills you have already taught them, such as dribbling while running,

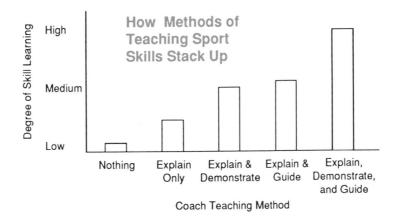

How Methods of Teaching Sport Skills Stack Up

(y-axis: Degree of Skill Learning — High, Medium, Low)
(x-axis: Coach Teaching Method — Nothing; Explain Only; Explain & Demonstrate; Explain & Guide; Explain, Demonstrate, and Guide)

switching dribbling hands while keeping their head up, and planting and pushing off a foot to change direction.

4. After players have demonstrated their ability to perform the separate parts of the skill in sequence, reexplain the entire skill.
5. Have them practice the skill.

Attend to Players Practicing the Skill

If the skill you selected was within your players' capabilities and you have done an effective job of introducing, demonstrating, and explaining it, your players should be ready to attempt the skill. Some players may need to be physically guided through the movements during their first few attempts at the skill. For example, some players may need your hands-on help to grip the ball and position their arms properly on their initial shot attempts. "Walking" unsure athletes through the skill in this

way will help them gain confidence to perform the skill on their own.

Your teaching duties don't end when all your athletes have demonstrated that they understand how to perform the skill. In fact, a significant part of your teaching will involve observing closely the hit-and-miss, trial performances of your players. As you observe players' efforts in drills and activities, offer positive, corrective feedback in the form of the "compliment sandwich" described in unit 3. If a player performs the skill properly, acknowledge it and offer praise. Keep in mind that your feedback will have a great influence on your players' motivation to practice and improve their performance.

Remember too that young players need individual instruction. So set aside a time before, during, or after practice to give them individual help.

What Planning Do I Need to Do?

Beginning coaches often make the mistake of showing up for the first practice with no particular plan in mind. These coaches find that their practices are unorganized, their players are frustrated and inattentive, and the amount and quality of their skill instruction is limited. Planning is essential to successful teaching *and* coaching. And it doesn't begin on the way to practice!

Preseason Planning

Effective coaches begin planning well before the start of the season. Among the preseason

measures that will make the season more enjoyable, successful, and safe for you and your players are the following:

- Familiarize yourself with the sport organization you are involved in, especially its philosophy and goals regarding youth sport.
- Examine the availability of facilities, equipment, instructional aids, and other materials needed for practices and games.
- Check to see that you have liability insurance through the sport organization to cover you when one of your players is hurt (see unit 5). If you don't, get some.
- Establish your coaching priorities regarding having fun, developing players' skills, and winning.
- Select and meet with your assistant coaches to discuss the philosophy, goals, team rules, and plans for the season.
- Register players for the team. Have them complete a player information form and obtain medical clearance forms, if required.
- Institute an injury-prevention program for your players.
- Hold a parent orientation meeting to inform parents of your background, philosophy, goals, and instructional approach. Also, give a brief overview of the league's

rules and basketball rules, terms, and strategies to familiarize parents or guardians with the sport.

You may be surprised at the number of things you should do even before the first practice. But if you address them during the preseason, the season will be much more enjoyable and productive for you and your players.

In-Season Planning

Your choice of activities during the season should be based on whether they will help your players develop physical and mental skills, knowledge of rules and game tactics, sportsmanship, and love for the sport. All of these goals are important, but we'll focus on the skills and tactics of basketball to give you an idea of how to itemize your objectives.

Goal Setting

What you plan to do during the season must be reasonable for the maturity and skill level of your players. In terms of basketball skills and tactics, you should teach young players the basics and move on to more complex activities only after they have mastered these easier techniques and strategies.

To begin the season, your instructional goals might include the following:

- Players will be able to assume and maintain the ready position.
- Players will be able to dribble with either hand.
- Players will be able to shoot a layup correctly from both sides of the basket.
- Players will be able to make accurate chest and bounce passes to stationary and moving teammates.
- Players will be able to catch passes while stationary or moving.
- Players will be able to maintain control of the dribble while running.
- Players will be able to set effective screens on the ball and away from the ball.
- Players will be able to position themselves and slide their feet to guard an opposing dribbler.
- Players will be able to position themselves correctly to guard opponents away from the ball.
- Players will be able to perform a set or jump shot using correct shooting technique.
- Players will demonstrate knowledge of basketball rules.
- Players will demonstrate knowledge of basic offensive and defensive strategies.

Organizing

After you've defined the skills and tactics you want your players to learn during the season, you can plan how to teach them to your players in practices. But be flexible! If your players are having difficulty learning a skill or tactic, take some extra time until they get the hang of it—even if that means moving back your schedule. After all, if your players are unable to perform the fundamental skills, they'll never execute the more complex skills you have scheduled for them.

Still, it helps to have a plan for progressing players through skills during the season. The 4-week sample of a season plan in Appendix A shows how to schedule your skill instruction in an organized and progressive manner. If this is your first coaching experience, you may wish to follow the plan as it stands. If you have some previous experience, you may want to modify the schedule to better fit the needs of your team.

What Makes Up a Good Practice?

A good instructional plan makes practice preparation much easier. Have players work on more important and less difficult goals in early season practice sessions. And see to it that players master basic skills before moving on to more advanced ones.

It is helpful to establish *one objective* for each practice; but try to include a *variety of activities* related to that objective. For example, although your primary objective might be to improve players' dribbling skill, you should have players perform several different drills designed to enhance that single skill. And, to interject further variety into your practices, vary the order of the activities you schedule.

In general, we recommend that each of your practices include the following:

- *Warm up*
- *Practice previously taught skills*
- *Teach and practice new skills*
- *Practice under competitive conditions*
- *Cool down*
- *Evaluate*

Warm Up

As you're checking the roster and announcing the performance objectives for the practice, your players should be preparing their bodies for vigorous activity. A 5- to 10-minute period of easy-paced activities (e.g., half-speed, full-court dribbling and layups), stretching, and calisthenics should be sufficient for youngsters to limber their muscles and reduce the risk of injury.

Practice Previously Taught Skills

Devote part of each practice to having players work on the fundamental skills they already know. But remember, kids like variety. So organize and modify drills to keep everyone involved and interested. Praise and encourage players when you notice improvement, and offer individual assistance to those who need help.

Teach and Practice New Skills

Gradually build on your players' existing skills by giving them something new to practice each session. The proper method for teaching sport skills is described on pages 19 to 21. Refer to those pages if you have any questions about teaching new skills or if you want to evaluate your teaching approach periodically during the season.

Practice Under Competitive Conditions

Competition among teammates during practices prepares players for actual games and informs young athletes about their abilities relative to those of their peers. Youngsters also seem to have more fun in competitive activities.

You can create contest-like conditions by using competitive drills, modified games, and scrimmages (see units 7 and 8). However, consider the following guidelines before introducing competition into your practices.

- All players should have an equal opportunity to participate.
- Match players by ability and physical maturity.
- Make certain players can execute fundamental skills before they compete in groups.
- Emphasize performing well, not winning, in every competition.
- Give players room to make mistakes by avoiding constant evaluation of their performances.

Cool Down

Each practice should wind down with a 5- to 10-minute period of light exercise, including jogging, performance of simple skills, and some stretching. The cool-down allows athletes' bodies to return to the resting state and avoid stiffness, affording you an opportunity to review the practice.

Evaluate

At the end of practice spend a few minutes with your players reviewing how well the session accomplished the objective you had set. Even if your evaluation is negative, show optimism for future practices and send players off on an upbeat note.

How Do I Put a Practice Together?

Simply knowing the six practice components is not enough. You must also be able to arrange those components into a logical progression and fit them into a time schedule. Now, using your instructional goals as a guide for selecting what skills to have your players work on, try to plan several basketball practices you might conduct. The following example should help you get started.

Sample Practice Plan

Performance Objective. Players will be able to throw effective chest and bounce passes.

Component	Time	Activity or drill
Warm up	10 min	Full-court dribbling Calisthenics
Practice	20 min	Shell drill Shark drill
Teach	15 min	2-hand chest and bounce passing with a partner, stationary and running full-court
Scrimmage	15 min	3-on-3 scrimmage
Cool down and evaluate	10 min	Easy jogging Free throws Stretching

Summary Checklist

During your basketball season, check your teaching and planning skills periodically. As you gain more coaching experience, you should be able to answer "Yes" to each of the following.

When you teach sport skills to your players, do you

____ arrange the players so all can see and hear?

____ introduce the skill clearly and explain its importance?

____ demonstrate the skill properly several times?

____ explain the skill simply and accurately?

____ attend closely to players practicing the skill?

____ offer corrective, positive feedback or praise after observing players' attempts at the skill?

When you plan, do you remember to plan for

____ preseason events like player registration, liability protection, use of facilities, and parent orientation?

____ season goals such as the development of players' physical skills, mental skills, sportsmanship, and enjoyment?

____ practice components such as warm up, practice previously taught skills, teach and practice new skills, practice under game-like conditions, cool down, and evaluate?

UNIT 5

What About Safety?

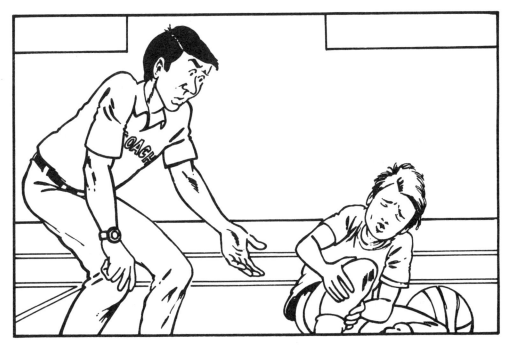

One of your players breaks free downcourt, dribbling the ball toward the basket for an apparent layup. But out of nowhere races a defender, who catches up with and accidentally undercuts the goal-bound player. You see that your player is not getting up and seems to be in pain. What do you do?

One of the least pleasant aspects of coaching is observing players get hurt. Fortunately, there are many preventive measures coaches can institute to reduce the risk. But in spite of such efforts, injury remains a reality of sport participation. Consequently, you must be prepared to provide first aid when injuries occur

and to protect yourself against unjustified lawsuits. This unit will describe how you can

- create the safest possible environment for your players,
- provide emergency first aid to players when they get hurt, and
- protect yourself from injury liability.

How Do I Keep My Players From Getting Hurt?

Injuries may occur because of poor preventive measures. Part of your planning, described in unit 4, should include steps that give your players the best possible chance for injury-free participation. These steps include the following:

- *Preseason physical examination*
- *Physical conditioning*
- *Apparel and facilities inspection*
- *Matching athletes by physical maturity and warning of inherent risks*
- *Proper supervision and record keeping*
- *Warm-up and cool-down*

Preseason Physical Examination

In the absence of severe injury or ongoing illness, your players should have a physical examination every 2 years. If a player has a known complication, a physician's consent should be obtained before participation is allowed. You should also have players' parents or guardians sign a participation agreement form and a release form to allow their son or daughter to be treated in the case of an emergency.

Physical Conditioning

Muscles, tendons, and ligaments unaccustomed to vigorous and long-lasting physical activity are prone to injury. Therefore, prepare your athletes to withstand the exertion of playing basketball. An effective conditioning program would include running, cutting, and jumping activities.

Make conditioning drills and activities fun. Include a skill component, such as dribbling or passing, to prevent players from becoming bored or looking upon the activity as "work." And don't forget, even the best conditioned athletes need rest and water breaks. So make sure water is available to your players and that you give them time to catch their breath during the practice session.

Apparel and Facilities Inspection

Another means to prevent injuries is to check the quality and fit of the clothes worn by your players. Slick-soled, poor-fitting, or unlaced basketball shoes, unstrapped eyeglasses, and jewelry are dangerous on the basketball court —both to the player wearing such items and to other participants. Encourage players to switch into their basketball shoes when they reach practice and game sites so that the soles of their shoes are free of mud and moisture.

Remember to examine regularly the court on which your players practice and play. Wipe up wet spots, remove hazards, report conditions you cannot remedy, and request maintenance as necessary.

INFORMED CONSENT FORM

I hereby give my permission for _____ to participate in

_____ during the athletic season beginning in 199___. Further, I authorize the school to provide emergency treatment of an injury to or illness of my child if qualified medical personnel consider treatment necessary *and* perform the treatment. This authorization is granted only if I cannot be reached and a reasonable effort has been made to do so.

Date _____ Parent or guardian _____

Address _____ Phone (___) _____

Family physician _____ Phone (___) _____

Pre-existing medical conditions (e.g., allergies or chronic illnesses) _____

_____

Other(s) to also contact in case of emergency _____

Relationship to child _____ Phone (___) _____

My child and I are aware that participating in _____ is a potentially hazardous activity. I assume all risks associated with participation in this sport, including but not limited to falls, contact with other participants, the effects of the weather, traffic, and other reasonable risk conditions associated with the sport. All such risks to my child are known and understood by me.

I understand this informed consent form and agree to its conditions on behalf of my child.

Child's signature _____ Date _____

Parent's signature _____ Date _____

Matching Athletes by Physical Maturity and Warning of Inherent Risks

Children of the same age may differ in height and weight by up to 6 inches and 50 pounds. That's why in contact sports and sports in which size provides an advantage, as in basketball, it's essential to match players against opponents of similar physical maturity and size. Such an approach gives smaller, less mature children a better chance to succeed and avoid injury, and provides larger children more of a challenge. Experience, ability, and emotional maturity are additional important factors to keep in mind when pairing athletes against each other.

Matching helps protect you from certain liability concerns. But you also must warn players of the inherent risks involved in playing basketball, because "failure to warn" is one of the most successful arguments in lawsuits against coaches. So, thoroughly explain the inherent risks of basketball and make sure each player knows, understands, and appreciates those risks.

ACEP Fact

Basketball is one of the top four injury-producing sports participated in by young athletes.

The preseason parent-orientation meeting is a good opportunity to explain the risks of the sport to parents and players. It is also a good opportunity to have both the players and their parents sign waivers releasing you from liability were an injury to occur. Such waivers do not relieve you of responsibility for your players' well-being, but they are recommended by lawyers.

Proper Supervision and Record Keeping

With youngsters, your presence in the area of play is not enough; you must actively plan and direct team activities and closely observe and evaluate players' participation. You're the watchdog responsible for their welfare. So if you notice a player limping or grimacing, give him or her a rest and examine the extent of the injury.

As a coach, you're also required to enforce the rules of the sport, prohibit dangerous horseplay, and hold practices only under safe weather conditions. These specific supervisory activities will make the play environment safer for your players and help protect you from liability in the event of an injury.

For further protection, keep records of your season plans, practice plans, and players' injuries. Season and practice plans come in handy when you need evidence that players have been taught certain skills, whereas accurate, detailed accident report forms offer protection against unfounded lawsuits. Ask for these forms from the organization to which you belong, and then hold onto them for several years so an "old basketball injury" of a former player doesn't come back to haunt you.

Warm-Up and Cool-Down

Although young bodies are generally very limber, they too can get tight from inactivity. Therefore, a warm-up period of approximately 10 minutes before each practice is strongly recommended. Warm-up should address each muscle group and get the heart rate elevated in preparation for strenuous activity. Easy running followed by stretching activities is a common sequence.

As practice is winding down, slow players' heart rates with an easy jog or walk. Then arrange for a 5- to 10-minute period of easy stretching at the end of practice to help players avoid stiff muscles and make them less tight before the next practice.

What If One of My Players Gets Hurt?

No matter how good and thorough your prevention program, injuries will occur. And when injury does strike, chances are you will be the one in charge. The severity and nature of the injury will determine how actively involved you'll be in treating the injury. But regardless of how seriously a player is hurt, it is your responsibility to know what steps to take. So let's look at how you can provide *basic* emergency care to your injured athletes.

ACEP Fact

Approximately 40% of all injuries in boys basketball involve players' ankles and feet.

Minor Injuries

Although no injury seems minor to the person experiencing it, most injuries are neither life-threatening nor severe enough to restrict participation. When such injuries occur, you can take an active role in their initial treatment.

Scrapes and Cuts

When a player has an open wound, follow these three steps:

1. Stop the bleeding by applying direct pressure with a clean dressing to the wound and elevating it. *Do not* remove the dressing if it becomes blood-soaked. Instead, place an additional dressing on top of the one already in place. If bleeding continues, elevate the injured area above the heart and maintain pressure.

2. Cleanse the wound thoroughly once the bleeding is controlled. A good rinsing with a forceful stream of water, and perhaps light scrubbing with soap will help prevent infection.

3. Protect the wound with sterile gauze or a band-aid. If the player continues to participate, apply protective padding over the injured area.

For bloody noses not associated with serious facial injury, have the athlete sit and lean slightly forward. Then pinch the player's nostrils shut. If the bleeding continues after several minutes or if the athlete has a history of nosebleeds, seek medical assistance.

Sprains and Strains

The physical demands of basketball practices and games often result in injury to the muscles or tendons (strains), or to the ligaments (sprains). When your players suffer minor strains or sprains, immediately apply the RICE method of injury care.

Bumps and Bruises

Inevitably, basketball players make contact with each other and with the hard court surface. And if the force of a body part at impact is great enough, a bump or bruise will result. Many players will continue playing with such sore spots, but if the bump or bruise is large and painful, you should act appropriately. Enact the RICE formula for injury care and monitor the injury. If swelling, discoloration, and pain have lessened, the player may resume participation with protective padding; if not, the player should be examined by a physician.

Serious Injuries

Head, neck, and back injuries, fractures, and injuries that cause a player to lose consciousness are among a class of injuries that you can-

The RICE Method

R—Rest the area to avoid further damage and foster healing.

I —Ice the area to reduce swelling and pain.

C—Compress the area by securing an ice bag in place with an elastic wrap.

E—Elevate the injury above heart level to keep the blood from pooling in the area.

not and *should not try to treat* yourself. But you *should plan* what you'll do if such an injury occurs. And your plan should include the following guidelines for action:

- Obtain the phone number and ensure the availability of nearby emergency care units.
- Assign an assistant coach or another *adult* the responsibility of contacting emergency medical help upon your request.
- *Do not move* the injured athlete.
- Calm the injured athlete and keep others away from him or her as much as possible.
- Evaluate whether the athlete's breathing is stopped or irregular, and if necessary, clear the airway with your fingers.
- If breathing has stopped, administer artificial respiration.
- If the athlete's circulation has stopped, administer cardiopulmonary resuscitation (CPR), or have a trained individual administer CPR.
- Remain with the athlete until medical personnel arrive.

ACEP Fact

Nearly 90% of girls' basketball injuries that require surgery involve the knee.

How Do I Protect Myself?

When one of your players is injured, naturally your first concern is his or her well-being. Your feelings for children, after all, are what made you decide to coach. Unfortunately, there is something else that you must consider: Can you be held liable for the injury?

From a legal standpoint, a coach has nine duties to fulfill. We've discussed all but planning (see unit 4) in this unit.

1. Provide a safe environment.
2. Properly plan the activity.
3. Provide adequate and proper equipment.
4. Match or equate athletes.
5. Warn of inherent risks in the sport.
6. Supervise the activity closely.
7. Evaluate athletes for injury or incapacity.
8. Know emergency procedures and first aid.
9. Keep adequate records.

In addition to fulfilling these nine legal duties, you should check your insurance coverage to make sure your present policy will protect you from liability.

Summary Self-Test

Now that you've read how to make your coaching experience safe for your players and yourself, test your knowledge of the material by answering these questions:

1. What are six injury prevention measures you can institute to try to keep your players from getting hurt?
2. What is the three-step emergency care process for cuts?
3. What method of treatment is best for minor sprains and strains?
4. What steps can you take to manage serious injuries?
5. What are the nine legal duties of a coach?

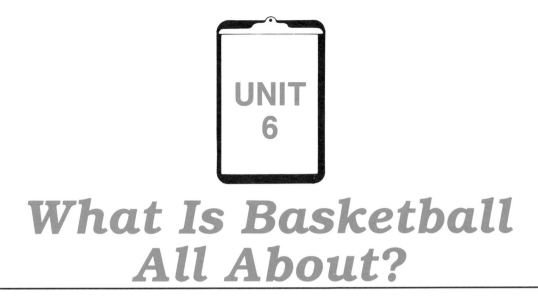

UNIT 6

What Is Basketball All About?

BASKETBALL MADE EASY!!

From reading the first part of this manual you now have a good general understanding of what it takes to coach. Now it's time to develop your comprehension of basketball. This part of the book provides the basketball-specific information you will need to teach your players the sport.

Basketball Coaching: Worth a Shot

You probably played or watched basketball before you agreed to coach it. But whether you were a high school star or an infrequent observer, you'll need a new perspective on the sport to teach it effectively to young players. If you were a player, you had to be concerned about only one role on the team—your own. Now you must consider not only your own coaching role, but *every* player's role on the team. Furthermore, you must help all of your players to learn and fulfill their roles.

So, why take the time and trouble to coach basketball? Perhaps the best reason is that kids love the sport. Give youngsters a basketball and a hoop, and they'll play until they drop. Kids' fondness for the sport is both a plus and a minus, though, in your effort to coach them. On the plus side, their interest and previous experience playing the sport should make them eager and somewhat prepared students of the game. On the minus side, having watched older, bigger, and much more skilled players perform, the youngsters may think they know more about the skills and strategies of the sport than they actually do know. Therefore, they may be less motivated to learn the basics of the sport.

ACEP Fact

United States' youths rank basketball as their #1 team sport.

Your challenge as a youth basketball coach is to inform your players well in the fundamentals of the sport and to maintain their attention and interest, *while still allowing them to have fun*. To meet this challenge, read the rest of this manual and then take your players to the HOOP:

H—Hold their attention with brief instruction and lots of activity.

O—Organize practices so players can both learn and have fun.

O—Opt for fulfilling players' needs rather than winning at all costs.

P—Provide a good model in skill demonstrations and courtside behavior.

What Are the Rules?

Basketball rules vary slightly at each level of play. Modifications are made to suit the size, skill, and age of the participants. Your team will play by rules similar to those established by the National Federation of State High School Associations, but check with the directors of your league before the season to learn of any unique guidelines they may have instituted. If you do your homework and communicate the rules well to your team, your players won't be caught unaware in games.

Ball and Court Dimensions

Because basketball is a game in which a ball is passed, dribbled, and shot with the hands, the size of the ball must be appropriate for participants. A regulation men's basketball is

far too heavy and large for kids to handle. Your league will probably use a standard women's basketball (18 to 20 ounces and 28.5 to 29.0 inches in circumference), or an even smaller ball that is made specifically for youth leagues.

Scaled-down courts let kids compete without getting too tired. We also recommend lowering the basket height, so that even the youngest players can get the ball to the hoop by shooting, not throwing, the ball—and experience success.

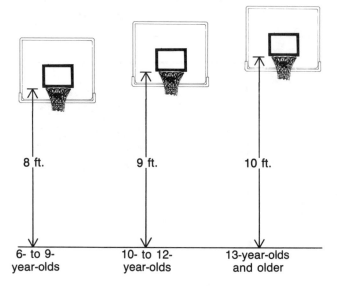

Recommended basket heights for youth basketball

8 ft.	9 ft.	10 ft.
6- to 9-year-olds	10- to 12-year-olds	13-year-olds and older

Court Markings

Regardless of the size of the court, specific areas of the floor are designated for certain game activities or restrictions. For instance, the free throw lane indicates where offensive players can spend no more than 3 seconds consecutively while their team is in control of the ball. Take time to familiarize yourself with the court markings illustrated in Figure 6.1.

Several areas of the court are referred to with special basketball terminology. The term *front-court* refers to the half of the court where your team's basket is located. The *backcourt* includes the midcourt line and the half of the court where your opponent's basket is located. The circle around the free throw line is called the *key*, and the point where the circle is farthest from the basket is referred to as the *top of the key*. The semicircle formed from the top of the key to the baseline is the *perimeter* area. Finally, the square marking 6 feet from the baseline on each side of the lane is referred to as the *block*.

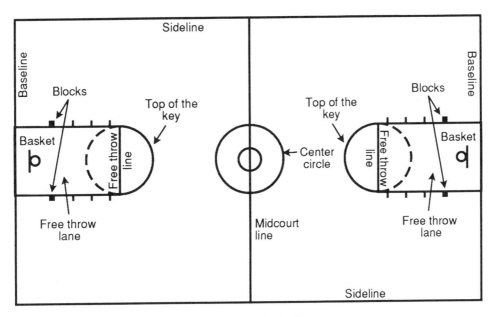

Figure 6.1 Basketball court.

Player Equipment

Basketball requires very little equipment. Basketball shoes are necessary for proper traction on the court, and two pairs of tube socks are recommended to avoid blisters. Athletic shorts and tank tops or loose-fitting shirts allow players the freedom of movement needed to run, jump, and shoot. Soft pads may be advised for players with conditions involving the knees or elbows. Safety glasses or goggles may be worn to protect eyes from injury.

Player Positions

Basketball is played with 5 players per team (although some youth leagues play 3-on-3). During the course of a game, each player alternates between offense (when the player's own team has the ball and is trying to score a basket) and defense (when the opposing team has the ball, and the player's team is trying to steal the ball and prevent the other team from scoring). The three general positions in basketball are commonly classified as guard, forward, and center (see Figure 6.2).

Guards

Guards usually are the best ballhandlers and outside shooters on the team. They tend to be shorter and quicker than the other players and have good dribbling and passing skills. Guards play farthest away from the basket, on the perimeter.

A basketball team usually has two guards in the game at all times. The point guard or #1 position is filled by the team's best dribbler and passer. The other guard position, the off guard or #2 position, is commonly given to the team's best long-range shooter and second-best dribbler.

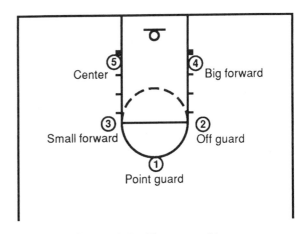

Figure 6.2 Player positions.

Forwards

Forwards typically are taller than guards and are stationed nearer the basket. Forwards should be able to shoot the ball accurately from within 12 feet of the basket and rebound the ball when shots are missed. Because of these responsibilities, forwards tend to stay near the free throw lane on offense.

A team usually plays with two forwards in its lineup. The small forward or #3 position is often filled by the most versatile and athletic member of the team. The small forward must be able to play in the lane and on the perimeter on offense, and to guard small and quick, or big and strong opponents on defense. The other forward position, the big forward or #4 position, is a good spot to assign to one of your bigger players and better rebounders who can also shoot the ball accurately from anywhere in the free throw lane.

Center

The center or #5 position, also referred to as the post, is frequently given to one of the tallest or biggest players on the team. That extra size is helpful for maneuvering for shots or rebounds around the basket. A tall center can also make it difficult for opposing teams to shoot near the basket. A center should have "soft" hands to catch the passes thrown into the lane area by guards and forwards. Most basketball teams designate one player on the court as their center.

Alternating Positions

Below the high school level, players should be given an opportunity to play more than one position. Obviously, you're not likely to play your smallest guard at center. And if you constantly shuffle players from one spot to another, they'll get confused. However, that doesn't mean you should have players stay at one position through the whole season.

Below is a sample system for alternating players among positions:

Primary position	Alternate position(s)
#1—Point guard	Off guard
#2—Off guard	Small forward, point guard
#3—Small forward	Off guard, big forward
#4—Big forward	Center, small forward
#5—Center	Big forward

Officials

A basketball game should be officiated by two or three individuals who know all the rules and enforce them to ensure a safe, fair, and fun contest. Officials should also require sportsmanship from all players *and* their coaches. You can be a big help to officials by acting with character and emphasizing to your players the need to play with discipline.

Appendix B shows the signals used by basketball officials during a game. Familiarize yourself with these signals and teach them to your players.

Length of the Game

Basketball games consist of two halves or four quarters, with intermissions of varying lengths. The game clock is stopped during these rest breaks, during time-outs, when the ball goes out of bounds, and when free throws are attempted. The length of the game should be adjusted according to the ages of the players. Youngsters 12 years old or under should play halves of no longer than 12 minutes. However, many youth leagues allow the clock to run continuously (except during time-outs and foul shots), so they play 16- to 20-minute halves.

Starting and Restarting the Game

A *jump ball* at center court is used to start games and overtime periods, which are played when teams are tied at the end of regulation time. During jump balls, each team has its center or best leaper attempt to tip the ball to a teammate (who must be outside of the center circle) to gain possession of the ball. In other jump ball situations, such as simultaneous possession of the ball by players from opposing teams, teams alternate possessions; the team that did not win the first jump ball takes the ball out of bounds in the next jump ball situation.

Play stops not only during intermissions and time-outs, but also when the ball goes out of bounds and when an official calls a violation or foul. The clock restarts when the ball is touched following an inbounds pass or a missed free throw. Whether the ball is inbounded or free throws are awarded depends on whether a violation or a foul was called; and, if a foul was called, whether (a) the team of the player who was guilty of the foul had used up its allotment of nonshooting team fouls for the quarter (usually 4 fouls) or half (usually 6 fouls), and

(b) the foul was made on a player who was in the act of shooting.

Fouls

Basketball is a contact sport, with 10 players often in close proximity in constant motion—running, cutting, and jumping. The rules of the game discourage rough play or tactics that allow a team to gain an advantage through brute strength. Therefore, fouls are most often called for what the officials perceive to be illegal physical contact between two or more players based on these general principles:

- The first player to establish position (to become stationary or set) on the court has priority rights to that position.
- A body part cannot be extended into the path of an opponent.
- The player who moves into the path of an opponent—especially an airborne opponent—when contact occurs is responsible for the contact.
- All players have the right to all of the space extending straight up from their feet on the floor. This is call the *principle of verticality*.

Types of Fouls

Based on the general principles concerning player contact, these specific fouls are called in a game:

Blocking—physically impeding the progress of another player while still moving

Charging—running into or pushing a defender who is stationary

Holding—restricting movement of an opponent

Illegal screen—a form of blocking, in that the player setting the screen is still moving when the defender makes contact

Over-the-back—infringing on the vertical plane of, and making contact with, a player who is in position and attempting to rebound

Reaching in—extending an arm and making contact with a ballhandler in an attempt to steal the ball

Tripping—extending a leg or foot and causing an opponent to lose balance and/or fall

The fouls listed are *personal* fouls. Certainly, this list is not all-inclusive, but it describes the most common kinds of fouls your players are likely to commit. The other fouls commonly committed in youth basketball are *shooting* fouls, where a defender makes contact with a player who is shooting the basketball. Emphasize to your players the importance of keeping hands off of the shooter, establishing position, using feet more than arms to play defense, and not attempting to rebound over an opponent.

Officials may also call *intentional, technical,* or *flagrant* fouls. If you have been a good role model for your players and have communicated effectively to them the importance of proper conduct on and off the court, your kids should not be cited for these types of fouls.

Consequences of Fouls

A team that fouls too much pays for it. Fouls carry with them increasingly severe penalties. A player with five fouls is disqualified from the game. And a team with more than a specified amount of fouls in a quarter or half gives the opposing team a *bonus* situation, allowing it to shoot "one-and-one" free throws (FTs) for nonshooting fouls. (If the first FT is made, a second shot is awarded the shooter; if the first attempt is missed, play continues with the rebound of the shot.)

This simple chart lists the types of fouls and their consequences:

Type of foul	Team fouled in bonus	Penalty
Shooting	Yes/No	Two FTs
Personal	No	Ball out of bounds
Personal	Yes	One-and-one FTs
Intentional	Yes/No	Two FTs
Technical	Yes/No	Two FTs and ball out of bounds
Flagrant	Yes/No	Two FTs, fouler is disqualified, ball out of bounds

Communicating After Fouls

How you discuss fouls with players is important. Some coaches at the college and professional levels instruct their players to "get physical" with opponents. Such advice is inappropriate for youths. Discourage rough and dirty play. On the other hand, don't inhibit your players by making them fearful of fouling. Hustling young players will inevitably pick up some fouls in each game. When a foul is called, point out to the guilty player why the violation was called and explain to the player how the foul could have been avoided with a more effective action.

Violations

Ballhandling and time violations occur three to four times more often than fouls in youth basketball. And the turnovers (loss of the ball to the defense) caused by these violations will be one of your continuing frustrations as a basketball coach.

Ballhandling Violations

Here is a list of common miscues committed by young ballhandlers:

Double dribble—resuming dribbling after having stopped dribbling (and no defender interrupts the player's possession of the ball) or dribbling with both hands at the same time

Charging—described as a foul previously, but also recorded as a turnover by the offense

Over-and-back—returning of the ball to the backcourt by the offensive team after it has crossed into the frontcourt, without the defense touching the ball

Traveling—taking more than one step without dribbling; also called "carrying the ball," and a variation of "turning the ball over" or "palming the ball" as a player turns the ball a complete rotation in the hand between dribbles

Time Violations

Basketball games have many time restrictions that you'll need to inform your players of. Here's a list of time violations you'll want them to avoid:

10 seconds in backcourt—The offensive team takes 10 or more seconds to get the ball across the midcourt line.

5 seconds inbound—The offensive team fails to throw the ball in within 5 seconds from the time the official hands the inbounder the ball. Time-outs must be called before the fourth count if a team is having trouble inbounding the ball.

5 seconds in possession—An offensive player fails to get rid of the ball within 5 seconds after being guarded within 6 feet by a defender in the frontcourt.

3 seconds in the lane—An offensive player is in the free throw lane of the frontcourt for 3 or more consecutive seconds while his or her team is in possession of the ball.

Other types of violations are possible, such as crossing the free throw line while shooting, or crossing the baseline or sideline while inbounding the ball. Most youth league officials do not get too picky about such violations, but make sure you inform your players of the proper guidelines. Then make sure they are performing according to the rules as they practice.

Communicating After Violations

John Wooden and other great basketball coaches have distinguished between errors of commission and errors of omission. Errors of commission are mistakes associated with effort, such as a foul committed while hustling for a loose ball. Unless players are playing out of control, don't correct them following errors of commission. On the other hand, errors of omission—failures to perform assigned duties or within the rules—must be brought to the attention of the guilty player. It may be that the player simply was unaware of the role or rule that was not fulfilled. Whatever the case, calmly explain to the player what is necessary to correct the performance.

Scoring

Two points (assuming no 3-point line) are awarded for every *field goal*—that is, for every shot made that is not a free throw. A made free throw is worth 1 point. The team that totals the most points over the course of the game is declared the winner.

Summary Test

Now that you've read the basic basketball information in this unit, you should be able to answer a number of questions about the sport. To test yourself, answer true (T) or false (F) to the following quiz questions.

1. _____ *Over-the-back* refers to a type of offensive turnover.
2. _____ The frontcourt is the half of the court where your team's basket is located.
3. _____ Personal fouls are the only type of fouls that are never penalized with a free throw.
4. _____ It is impossible for a team that makes fewer field goals than its opponent to win the game
5. _____ A player who jumps straight up with arms directly overhead should never be called for charging.
6. _____ Guards are usually most comfortable playing on the "blocks."
7. _____ A 5-second violation cannot be called if the inbounds passer calls a time-out between the fourth and fifth count.
8. _____ If two opponents make contact, either blocking or charging should be called.
9. _____ The player who is least likely to turn the ball over should be positioned at small forward.
10. _____ Basketball is an easier sport to teach than most because kids typically know the fundamentals.

Answers: 1. F   2. T   3. F   4. F   5. T   6. F   7. F   8. F   9. F   10. F

UNIT 7

What Basketball Skills and Drills Should I Teach?

In unit 4 you learned *how* to teach basketball skills and plan for practices. Now it's time to consider exactly *what* basketball skills to emphasize and what activities you'll use to help your players develop them. In this unit we'll describe the basic skills and recommend a variety of drills you can use to develop your players' basketball skills. These symbols will be used in figures throughout the remainder of the book to represent players, their movements, and the skills they are performing:

Defensive player	×
Offensive player	○
Offensive player with ball	●
Path of player	⟶
Path of pass	⇢
Path of dribble	⟿
Spot where ball is caught	●

41

What Basketball Skills Are Important?

This section describes the basic basketball skills you'll want your players to learn during the season. Remember, start with the most basic individual skills and slowly progress players through more difficult techniques. Monitor players' understanding of each new skill by asking them specific questions about the skill and watching them attempt to perform it. Then you won't lose them along the way as you advance your skill instruction.

Position and Movement

Many coaches take for granted their players' ability to position and move around the court. Don't! You'll save a lot of time and increase your players' effectiveness if you emphasize proper footwork in your first few practices.

The Ready Position

The most basic basketball skill is the ready position. Instruct your players to stand relaxed with arms and legs bent and weight shifted slightly forward to the balls of the feet (see Figure 7.1). From this position a player can

Figure 7.1   Ready position.

more easily run forward or backward, slide to either side, cut, pivot, and jump. So, from the very first practice, have your players assume and maintain an alert ready stance on the court.

Slides, Cuts, and Pivots

Young ballplayers often play as if their feet were glued to the court. Yet whether they're attempting to guard an opponent or get open to catch a pass, it's essential that they move their feet effectively. You can help them by showing them how to

- slide their feet without crossing them,
- push off a foot when running to cut quickly in another direction, and
- turn or pivot on the ball of one foot to change direction.

Slides.   Basketball defenders must be able to move swiftly from side to side. This movement is necessary to prevent offensive players from driving or cutting uncontested to the basket. It is also an effective move for offensive players who are being guarded from behind and are facing a teammate who has the ball. But youngsters are much more comfortable with forward than with lateral movement and thus tend to cross their feet when attempting to move sideways. Therefore, you will need to take time to teach and drill them to slide their feet effectively.

Instruct players to stand in the ready position and then move the leg nearest their intended direction about 2 feet to that side. Next they should slide the other foot until the feet once again are shoulder-width apart (see Figure 7.2). Remind players to keep their toes pointed forward and to move as quickly as possible on the balls of their feet. They'll be able to slide more quickly if they keep their knees bent, rears down, and backs erect.

Figure 7.2   Lateral slides.

Cuts. The ability to change direction quickly and in balance is important on both the offensive and the defensive end of the court. Offensive players will have trouble getting open for passes or shots if they cannot "lose" their opponents with quick cuts. And defenders will find it difficult to keep up with effective offensive players if they are unable to respond in kind to various cuts to get open.

Therefore, teach all of your players how to cut on the court by having them practice planting one foot on the court at the end of a stride, then pushing off that foot to shift their momentum in another direction. For example, tell players to push off with the left foot if they wish to cut to the right. Then they should turn the unplanted foot in the direction they want to go, and lead with that leg as they burst toward the new direction. Three very effective cuts used by offensive players to get open are the L-cut, V-cut, and backdoor cut (see Figure 7.3).

Pivots. Perhaps no other basic basketball skill is as lacking from the young player's repertoire as pivoting. Yet on defense and particularly on offense, players must be able to pivot effectively.

A pivot simply involves stopping, then turning one side of the body forward (front pivot) or backward (back pivot), all while keeping the ball of one foot on the court (see Figure 7.4). The stop and rotation components of pivoting are what distinguish it from cutting.

If you can get your players to pivot properly, you're ahead of the game; this is a skill that even some high school players have trouble performing. Even if your players do execute pivots well, remind them that they are limited to only one pivot foot each time they have the ball.

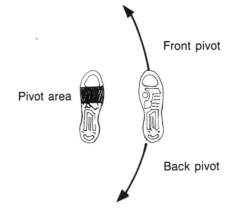

Figure 7.4   One foot pivot.

Slide, Cut, and Pivot Drills

Name.   **Lane Slide**

Purpose.   To improve lateral movement and footwork

Organization.   Two players are assigned to each free throw lane. One player has the ball at the free throw line. The other player in the pair is positioned on a block. The player with the ball rolls it to the block opposite the partner. The partner slides across the lane, retrieves the ball, and fires a quick chest pass to the player at the line. Upon receiving the return pass, the player at the free throw line rolls the ball to the opposite block, and the partner slides over to retrieve it. This sequence repeats until the player on the block has retrieved and returned 10 passes. Then players switch positions and repeat the drill.

Coaching Points.   Watch that the player on the block slides across the lane without crossing the feet. The player should maintain the ready

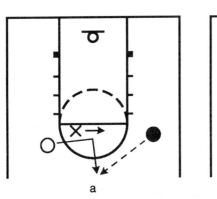

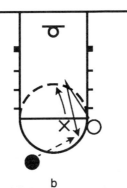

a   b   c

Figure 7.3   (a) L-cut, (b) V-cut, and (c) backdoor cut.

Error Detection and Correction for Pivoting

Young players often look unsure of how to move or turn without using the dribble when they have the basketball. Therefore, they need sound instruction on how to pivot with the ball.

ERROR

Moving and switching the pivot foot while in possession of the ball

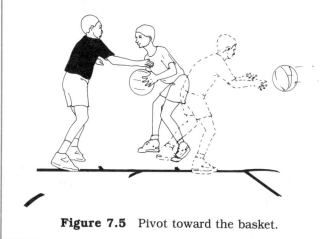

Figure 7.5 Pivot toward the basket.

CORRECTION

1. Tell players to always turn and face the basket as soon as they receive the ball (see Figure 7.5).

2. Instruct them to read their defenders to determine which foot to pivot on.

3. Remind players that once they choose a pivot foot, they cannot lift that foot from or slide it across the floor.

4. Encourage players to take full advantage of their ability to pivot in either direction as long as they keep the ball of the pivot foot in the same spot.

position throughout the drill. Emphasize good passes, with proper pace and location.

Variation. Double Lane Slide. Give the player at the free throw line another ball. Just as the player on the block is about to pass the first ball, the player at the line should roll the other ball to the opposite block. This will require the player on the block to slide quicker across the lane.

Name. **V-Cut and Layup**

Purpose. To teach players how to cut to get open and to convert layups when they are open

Organization. Six players are at each end of the court, three players on each wing. A coach is positioned at the top of the key at each end of the court and directs the drill as follows. The first player in each line has a ball and passes to the coach, then V-cuts and receives a return pass. After receiving the pass, the player pivots to face the hoop, then dribbles with the outside hand to the basket and shoots a layup. When the player begins the dribble to the basket, the player in the line on the opposite wing throws a pass to the coach and duplicates the movements of the first player. After shooting the layup, a player throws the ball to the first player in the opposite line and goes to the back of that line.

Coaching Points. Have players cut quickly, as if they are being guarded closely by a defender. Watch that they use proper catching and pivoting technique. Tell them to concentrate on driving hard to the hoop and shooting the layup correctly.

Variation. Backdoor and Layup. Same organization as above, except that after the player throws the pass to the coach, the player executes a backdoor cut and catches the pass on the way to the basket for a layup.

Name. **Catch and Pivot**

Purpose. To help players learn to move the ball effectively and pivot toward the basket as soon as they catch the ball

Organization. Two balls and six players at each end of the court, three players on each side of the half court. One player is on the block, another is at one side of the free throw line, and another has the ball on the foul line extended (the wing) near the sideline. The player on the wing passes overhead to the player on the free throw line, who pivots immediately toward the hoop and passes overhead to the player on the block, who also pivots toward the basket. The player on the block then pivots toward the corner and passes overhead to the wing player who has moved down to that position. The player who had been at the free throw line moves out to the wing to catch a pass from the corner (see Figure 7.6). Then the sequence is repeated, with the wing player passing to the player who has moved from the block to the end of the free throw line. After turning to the basket, this player throws a pass to the player on the block (who moved there from the corner).

Coaching Points. Look for good, crisp passing and quick pivots. See that players don't switch their pivot feet. Tell players to vary the direction of their pivots. Have players switch sides of the court after 3 minutes.

Variation. Catch, Pivot, and Shoot. The player on the block now makes a move to the hoop for a layup or shoots a jump shot off the backboard after pivoting. Have players vary the types of passes they throw.

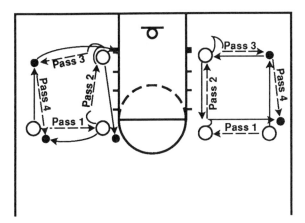

Figure 7.6 Catch and Pivot drill.

Ballhandling Skills

A key to success in basketball is moving the ball effectively from one player to another and getting into position to take high-percentage shots. Then, when the shot is there, players must be able to make it. Therefore the skills of passing, catching, dribbling, and shooting are essential to success in basketball.

Passing

Passing is an offensive skill used to maintain possession and create scoring opportunities. Passes should usually be short and crisp, because long or slow passes are likely to be stolen by an opposing player. However, players should avoid throwing too hard or using passes that are difficult to control. Passers should throw the ball above the waist and within easy reach of the receiver. If possible, passes should be thrown to the receiver's side that is farthest from her or his defender.

If your players become very skilled passers, work with them on faking a pass one way, then passing another. If they become very proficient, ask them to look away from the teammate to whom they are passing, to confuse the defense.

But keep it simple at the beginning by starting your players with these four types of passes:

- Chest pass
- Bounce pass
- Two-hand overhead pass
- Baseball pass

Chest Pass.   The chest pass, shown in Figure 7.7, is so named because the ball is thrown with two hands from the passer's chest to the receiver's chest area. This pass should have some zip on it, so the passer must have momentum *toward* the target. Also, teach your players to throw the pass with their thumbs down and moving through the ball as they release it. The ball will then have back-spin on it and will "bite" when caught by the receiver.

Figure 7.7 Two-hand chest pass.

Bounce Pass.   Sometimes it is easier for a passer to get the ball to a teammate by bouncing the ball once on the court before it reaches the receiver. For example, a defender may be guarding a player with both hands overhead, preventing a pass through the air to a teammate. In

Figure 7.8 Bounce pass.

that case a bounce pass may be the only route to get the ball to a teammate. Instruct your players to use bounce passes as a second option to air passes; the bounce slows down the ball, making it easier for defenders to steal.

When they do throw bounce passes, however, have them bounce the ball on the court two-thirds of the way between themselves and the receiver, as illustrated in Figure 7.8. This should get the ball to the receiver at waist level, the appropriate height for delivering this type of pass.

Two-Hand Overhead Pass.   Another pass option is the two-hand overhead pass. This pass is often a good way for a guard to get the ball in to a center or forward in the lane. It also is useful for throwing the ball over a group of players to a teammate on the other side of the court or downcourt on a fast break.

The pass must be thrown with a hand on each side, with the thumbs behind the ball. The ball need not be brought back far behind the head, but the passer must generate momentum toward the target and follow through with both arms extended. Tell your players to aim for the receiver's head, because the overhead pass often falls slightly short of its mark. That way, most of their passes should reach their teammate at chest height.

Baseball Pass.   The one-hand baseball pass is very difficult for youngsters to throw. They simply don't have large enough hands to get a good grip on the ball. However, if players are able to execute the pass, it is most beneficial when a player needs to get the ball to a team-

mate quickly over a distance greater than 20 feet.

Much as a baseball is pitched, this pass is thrown with the player's strongest arm and with significant force. The leg on the throwing-arm side serves as the push-off point for the forward momentum required for the pass (see Figure 7.9). After the player cocks the arm, the weight of the body should shift from the back (arm side) foot to the front foot. The index finger of the throwing hand should point directly toward the target as the ball is released, with the throwing arm following through completely.

Figure 7.9 Baseball pass.

Catching

Even the best passes are of little value if they aren't caught. And sloppy receiving technique is often the cause of turnovers and missed scoring opportunities. But if you emphasize and teach your players these receiving techniques, they should *catch on*:

- Move *to* the ball quickly but under control.
- Look the ball into the hands.
- Use two hands, grasping the ball tightly with the fingers and thumbs.

In most situations after receiving a pass, players should come to a stop with their feet positioned shoulder-width apart for balance. From this position, players should pivot to face the basket, looking for an open teammate, a shot, or a lane to dribble the ball to the basket. Catching passes on fast breaks is more difficult because a player's momentum will be toward the basket, not toward the pass, and it is much more difficult to control a pass while running downcourt at full speed. Stress to your players the importance of maintaining control—that they should never be moving so fast that they have to take more than one stride before being able to change direction.

Passing and Catching Drills

Name. **Partner Passing**

Purpose. To help players learn to pass and catch on the move

Organization. Have players pair up on the baseline in two lines, one line on each side of the free throw lane. Each player in one line has a ball. The pairs begin running downcourt under control, chest-passing the ball accurately and quickly to one another. The next pair should not begin until the previous pair is to the free throw line. When both lines have been down the court, have the last pair to finish turn around and start the same process down to the opposite end of the court.

Coaching Points. Emphasize making quick passes and using proper receiving techniques. See that players lead their partners with their passes so that partners do not have to slow down to catch them. Reinforce players for good passing and for avoiding bobbles or loose balls.

Variations. Partner Passing—Bounce Passes. Same as above, but players should bounce-pass the ball.

Partner Passing and Layup. Same as above except that the last player to receive a pass goes straight up for a layup.

Partner Passing and Jumper. Same as above except that the player who receives a pass within 12 feet of the hoop stops and goes straight up for a bank-shot jumper.

Name. **Hot Potato**

Purpose. To teach players to look away from players to whom they are passing and to react quickly in receiving passes

Organization. Six players at each end of the court. In each group, one player stands with a ball inside the top of the key, facing the

basket. The other five players position themselves in a semicircle from one side of the free throw line to the other, facing their teammate out front. One player among the five in the semicircle has a basketball. The drill begins with the player near the top of the key throwing a chest pass to one of the four players in the semicircle who do not have a basketball. As soon as this pass is made, the player in the semicircle who began the drill with a ball chest-passes to the player out front, who then chest-passes the ball again to another teammate (see Figure 7.10). This drill continues for 1 minute. Players then rotate clockwise so the player on the right side of the free throw line moves to the top of the key and the player at the top of the key moves to the left side of the free throw line.

Coaching Points. Emphasize quick and accurate passing. Timing is very important to the success of this drill, so one bobble can disrupt the entire passing/catching sequence. The player out front is forced to look away from the player to whom the pass is being made because attention must be devoted to receiving the next pass. Therefore, see to it that these "blind" passes are accurate—reaching the intended players in the chest area.

Variation. Hot Potato Bounce. Same as above, except that players bounce-pass the ball to one another.

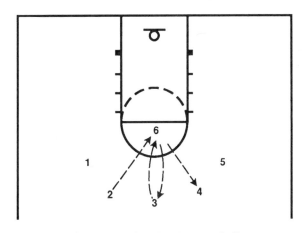

Figure 7.10 Hot Potato drill.

Name. **Pressure Passer**

Purpose. To improve players' ability to pass and pass-fake when guarded closely by a defender

Organization. Four groups of three players, with each group at a good distance from the others. Two offensive players in each group face each other, 10 to 12 feet apart. The third player is a defender, positioned between the offensive players, within 2 feet of the offensive player with the ball. One offensive player attempts to bounce- or chest-pass to the partner while the defender attempts to prevent the pass. Passers and receivers cannot move more than one step from their pivot feet, and passers cannot simply lob the ball over the defender's head. When a bad pass is thrown or the defender makes a steal, the player who passed the ball moves to the defensive position and the defender switches to offense. Each player should have a turn on defense before the drill is ended.

Coaching Points. Encourage offensive players to use fakes and read the defender when attempting a pass. Make sure players are not switching their pivot feet and that the passes they make are on the money. Finally, prompt defenders to hustle and overplay the passer's strong hand in their efforts to steal the ball.

Dribbling

If there's one thing that young players like to do when they get their hands on a basketball, it's to bounce it. Unfortunately, when they practice on their own, only a few players dribble correctly or use techniques that will improve their dribbling skill. Therefore, you'll need to teach your players how to dribble effectively and watch that they use the correct dribbling technique shown in Figure 7.11.

Figure 7.11 Correct dribbling technique.

Teaching players correct dribbling technique is problematic, because most of them have already established incorrect dribbling habits. The three most common errors of self-taught youth dribblers are these: slapping at the ball from the chest area and waiting for it to bounce back up; keeping the head down, with eyes riveted to each bounce; and using one hand exclusively to bounce the ball.

As you correct these dribbling errors and attempt to improve your players' dribbling skills, advise them to:

- Establish a feel for the ball, with the fingers and pad of the hand.
- Maintain the ready position, keeping knees bent and rear down.
- Always bounce the ball low to the court (below waist height), and even closer to the floor when being guarded.
- Bounce the ball close to the body.
- Keep the head up and see the rest of the court (and teammates!).
- Learn how to dribble with the right *and* left hand.
- Practice!

Dribbling Drills

Name. **Figure Eight**

Purpose. To teach players to control the ball with both hands and to look up while dribbling

Organization. Each player has a ball. Players spread out so that each has a radius of 3 feet of clear space in which to dribble. Players should all face the same direction, with the coach in front of them. The players bounce the balls in figure eights through and around their legs. When they have dribbled this pattern in one direction successfully for 1 minute, have them switch directions and dribble the same pattern for another minute.

Coaching Points. Test players for keeping their heads up while dribbling by raising a certain number of fingers at three times during each half of the drill. At the end of the first minute ask players what the three numbers were, and do the same for the second minute. Observe players' dribbling technique, making sure that they are keeping the ball close to the floor and are not slapping at the ball.

Variation. Monkey Drill. Organize players as above, but have players control the ball by

---

Dribbling Dos and Don'ts

Dribbling Dos

Do #1   Maintain the dribble until a pass or shot opportunity is created.

Do #2   Vary the speed and direction of the dribble so defenders cannot anticipate steal opportunities.

Do #3   Keep a ball-body-defender relationship when dribbling the ball near an opponent.

Do #4   Cross-over, or switch dribbling hands, after dribbling past an opponent to protect the ball.

Do #5   Stay in the middle areas of the court and away from the corners when dribbling, to avoid getting trapped.

Dribbling Don'ts

Don't #1   Don't automatically put the ball on the floor and begin dribbling immediately after receiving the ball, unless a layup opportunity is evident.

Don't #2   Don't pick up or stop the dribble with no apparent option (shot or pass) available.

Don't #3   Don't dribble into a crowd, because the ball is likely to be stolen.

Don't #4   Don't try to get fancy, when the basics of dribbling are difficult enough.

Don't #5   Don't hesitate, because an unsure dribbler is a turnover waiting to happen.

---

dribbling it between their legs in this sequence: right hand in front of legs, left hand in front of legs, right hand behind legs, left hand behind legs, and return to right hand in front of legs to start sequence again (see Figure 7.12).

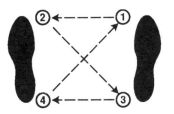

Figure 7.12   Monkey drill.

Name. **Whistle Dribble**

Purpose. To practice changing direction quickly and looking up while dribbling

Organization. Each player has a ball. Players spread out in the middle part of the court, all facing the same direction. Use a whistle to have them start dribbling and to have them change direction. Players should always face the coach, who points a basketball in the direction players are to dribble.

Coaching Points. Keep players guessing by varying the direction. Have players dribble with the right hand when going right and backward with the left hand when dribbling left and forward. Remind players to keep their heads up and to dribble low to the floor, especially when switching hands with the dribble.

Variation. Whistle Jump. Same as above, but whenever the whistle blows, players should grip the ball with both hands and jump straight up as high as they can with the ball overhead, then return to the floor in the ready position with the ball out in front of them, ready to dribble in either direction.

Shooting

Every player gets a kick out of putting the basketball through the hoop. So your players will be highly motivated to learn proper shooting technique *if* you convince them that it will help them make more of their shots.

To get the fundamentals of shooting across and encourage your players to learn them, tell them they'll SCORE if they do these things:

S—Select only high-percentage shots

C—Concentrate on the rim or backboard

O—Order movements: square up, bend knees and elbows, cock wrist

R—Release the ball using proper shooting mechanics

E—Extend the shooting arm toward the basket (follow through)

Players can shoot the ball in a variety of ways, including jump shots, set shots, free throws, and layups. Introduce your team to each variation, and emphasize the shots that they are most capable of executing at their stage of development.

Jump and Set Shots. Although the most common shot at most levels of play is the jump shot, young players who lack the leg strength to spring from the floor while shooting will more often shoot set shots. The jump and set shots differ only in the leg action involved—the jump shot requiring more knee bend and a forceful pushoff from the floor.

Teach your players these shooting mechanics in this sequence:

1. Lay the ball on the fingers and pads of each hand (they'll hold the ball too tightly if you tell them to grip it), with the shooting hand behind and slightly underneath the ball and the nonshooting hand balancing the ball from the side.

2. Focus on the rim or backboard. The middle of the rim should be the target on most shots, but when at a 30- to 60-degree angle from the hoop, sight the corner of the square of the backboard for a bankshot (see Figure 7.13).

3. Align shoulders, hips, and feet square to the basket. The foot on the shooting-hand side can be up to 6 inches in front of the other foot if that base of support is more comfortable.

4. Bend the knees to get momentum for

Figure 7.13 Sighting the basket.

the shot. Let the legs, not the arms, be the primary power source for the shot.

5. Bend the shooting-arm elbow to approximately a 90-degree angle, keeping the arm perpendicular to the floor and in front of the cocked wrist as the ball is brought up to the shooting position above the forehead (see Figure 7.14).

6. Jump straight up to a comfortable height off the floor, remaining square to the

Figure 7.14 Correct stance for the jump shot.

basket and maintaining the arm position described in Step 5.

7. Just prior to reaching the top of the jump, release the ball by extending the elbow, bringing the wrist forward, and moving the fingers of the shooting hand up and through the ball (see Figure 7.15). The nonshooting arm and hand should maintain their supportive position on the side of the ball until after the release.

8. Follow through after the release by landing square on both feet, extending the shooting arm even further forward, dropping the wrist, and pointing the index finger of the shooting hand directly at the basket.

For the first few practices your players will probably have difficulty shooting the ball properly. That's because they've developed

Figure 7.15 Proper ball release on the jump shot.

Error Detection and Correction for Shooting

Many kids take a dribble before every shot. This is a bad habit because it allows the defense to recover and prevent, pressure, or block the shot. So you'll want to break them of this routine and get them to shoot without putting the ball on the floor.

ERROR	CORRECTION
Dribbling before shooting when open, within good shooting range, or without a clear path to the basket	1. Receive the pass and pivot to face the basket.

2. Hold the ball in preparation for a shot or a two-handed pass.

3. Check where the defense is positioned, whether a shot is available, and whether a teammate closer to the basket is open (see Figure 7.16).

4. If the nearest defender does not deny the shot and no teammate is open for a higher percentage shot, shoot the ball.

Figure 7.16 Check possible options before shooting.

bad shooting habits and the correct shooting motion is awkward for them. Watch to be sure that your players aren't shooting line drives at the hoop. Such shots are not likely to go in the basket unless they are right on target. So monitor the arc of your players' shots; if the arc is at an appropriate height, a rim shot has a chance of going in.

Free Throws.   After shooting fouls, and when the team is in the bonus, the player fouled is awarded free throws. The free throw is nothing more than an uncontested set shot from a designated spot—the free throw line. Players should use the same shooting mechanics outlined for the jump and set shots. However, because free throw attempts are unhurried and uncontested, teach players to take a deep breath and take their time before shooting. Also encourage each of them to establish a free throw ritual before releasing the shot, such as dribbling the ball a certain number of times or saying something to build their confidence for the shot (e.g., "Net").

Layups.   The highest percentage shot, and therefore the most desirable shot, is a layup. However, with young and inexperienced players, layups are hardly "gimmes." So you'll need to work with your team on proper layup technique from both sides of the basket.

A layup is a one-handed shot taken within 3 feet of the basket (see Figure 7.17). Teach players to use their left hands when shooting layups from the left side of the basket and their right hands when shooting from the right side of the basket. The layup motion begins with the player planting and exploding (much like a high jumper) off the foot opposite the shooting hand, after striding directly to the hoop. The player explodes off the planted foot straight up into the air. At the top of the jump, the player releases the ball by bringing the shooting hand, which is underneath the ball and near the shoulder, up toward the basket. As in the jump and set shots, the index finger of the shooting hand should be pointed directly at the basket or the appropriate spot on the backboard.

Your right-handed players are likely to find left-handed layups troublesome, just as your left-handed players are going to find right-handed layups difficult. Point out to them the reason for using the hand farthest from the basket to shoot the ball: The ball is more easily

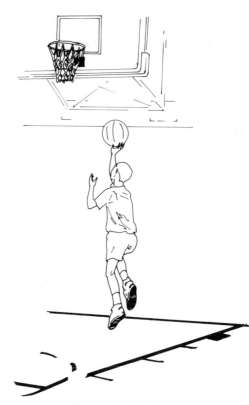

Figure 7.17   Layup.

protected and less easily blocked. Then walk them through the proper footwork and shooting motion from their unaccustomed sides. Once they get the mechanics down, they can speed up their drive to the hoop and shooting motion. Finally, as with all shots, your players must repeatedly practice *the proper technique.*

Shooting Drills

Name.   **Lay-In Stay In**

Purpose.   To get players to concentrate and use correct layup technique when shooting close to the basket

Organization.   Players are divided into two equal lines, one each side of the lane, facing the basket, with the first player in each line 15 to 18 feet from the hoop. The first two players in one line each have a basketball. The first player with a ball goes in and shoots a layup while the first player in the opposite line goes in to rebound. The second player in the shooting line with a ball drives to the hoop just as the first shooter begins to shoot. The player who rebounds the first shot passes the ball to the third player in the shooting line who is moving toward the basket. Players alternate between the rebounding and shooting lines. This sequence continues as long as no player misses. When a player misses, that player can serve only as a rebounder. The drill continues until all but one player has missed. Then the shooting line side is switched to the opposite side of the court and the same procedure is carried out.

Coaching Points. Look for proper technique. If players are worried more about making the basket than about shooting the layup properly and off the backboard, establish proper form as the criterion—not whether they make the basket.

Name. **Around the World**

Purpose. To improve shooting skill from various spots on the court and shooting without dribbling

Organization. If four baskets are available, assign three players to each hoop. Each group should have two basketballs. Two players in the group, each with a basketball, should be positioned near, but on opposite sides of, the basket. These players serve as rebounders for the third teammate, who shoots 10 consecutive shots from five designated spots that form a semicircle in front of the backboard. Beginning from a spot on the baseline, 12 to 15 feet from the basket, the shooter catches a pass from one of the rebounders and shoots a jump shot. The shooter then hustles to the next spot, receives a pass from the other rebounder, and goes up for another shot. By this time, the rebounder who threw the first pass will have retrieved that ball and can deliver a pass to the shooter, who has moved to the third spot on the floor—near the middle of the free throw line. This sequence continues until the shooter has shot from each of the five spots twice (see Figure 7.18). Then one of the rebounders takes the shooter's position and the shooter becomes a rebounder.

Coaching Points. Emphasize quick movement from one shooting position to the next. See that players are using proper shooting form and that the passes by the rebounders are accurate and timely.

Defensive Skills

The individual defensive skills of basketball are sometimes less appreciated than the individual

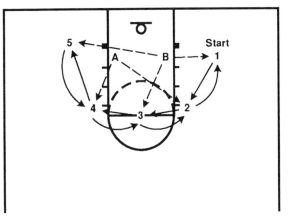

Figure 7.18   Around-the-World drill.

offensive techniques, but they are just as important. Kids need to learn the basics of player-to-player defense from the outset, if they are to compete successfully in drills, scrimmages, and games.

Moving the Feet

From the ready position, described on page 42, a defender can move quickly in any direction and maintain balance. Movement from this ready position is the key to a defensive player's success. A defender must move in short, quick, lateral bursts. Therefore, have your players practice sliding (as described on page 42) from one point to another quickly, *without* crossing one leg over the other.

Sometimes when an offensive player has gained an advantage by moving between the hoop and the defender, the defender must pivot and run to catch up and reestablish position. Even the best defensive players get beat momentarily. So emphasize to your players to keep their feet active on defense, with the objective of staying between their opponents and the basket, and, if they do get beat by an offensive player, to hustle back into position.

Guarding an Opponent With the Ball

Obviously, the reason for guarding offensive players with the ball is to prevent them from scoring. A defender can best accomplish this by staying between his or her assigned opponent and the basket, as shown in Figure 7.19. The closer the opponent is to the hoop, the closer the defender should guard the player.

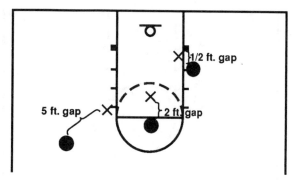

Figure 7.19   Correct defensive position on the ball.

Tell your players to consider these things about their bodies and court positions when guarding a player with the ball:

- Body position
  - *Are my arms up, ready to prevent an easy pass?*
  - *Am I in the ready position and alert?*
  - *Am I taking away the player's strong hand (e.g., overplaying to my left a right-handed opponent)?*

- Court position
  - *Is the player out of shooting range?*
  - *Am I close enough to the player to prevent an easy shot?*
  - *Am I too close, so the opponent can drive around me?*
  - *Will a teammate be able to help me if the player beats me with the dribble?*

Defenders against players with the ball should not be suckered in by fakes. Instruct your players to watch and move with the opponent's belly button; unlike the ball, feet, head, and shoulders, the waist of the player will move only when an actual movement is made. If an offensive player begins to dribble, your defensive player should make sure to cut off a direct drive to the hoop and try to get the player to pick up (stop) the dribble. Once the dribble stops, the defender should move up close to the offensive player with arms up to prevent a pass.

Have your players notice opponents' offensive habits with the ball, such as using only one hand to dribble, pass, or shoot. Then

---

Error Detection and Correction for Guarding Away From the Ball

Too often defensive players lose track of where their assigned offensive player is on the court. This happens because they're watching only the movement of the ball, not their player. You'll need to teach players how to position themselves so they can see *both* the player they are guarding and the ball.

ERROR

Defenders away from the ball losing track of where their offensive player is on the court

Figure 7.20   Mid-pointing player and ball.

CORRECTION

1. Have players establish ball-you-player position.

2. Instruct players to move toward the basket enough to be able to see both the ball and their player (see Figure 7.20).

3. Adjust position as the offensive player or ball changes position.

they'll be able to overplay the offensive players to whom they are assigned and perhaps steal or block the ball. However, tell your players to avoid reaching in for the ball against an opponent; what they'd come away with would more likely be a foul than the ball.

Guarding an Opponent Away From the Ball

If there is one thing you'll have trouble convincing players of, it's that it isn't nap time just because the player they're guarding does not have the ball. Just as when guarding a player with the ball, defenders should be in the ready position *and* alert.

A simple way to convey to players how to position themselves when they're guarding players who don't have the ball is to have them maintain a ball-you-player relationship. The farther the ball is away from the defender, the farther away from the offensive player the defender can play.

Defensive Drills

Name. **Cut Off the Cutter**

Purpose. To practice defending against players who are working hard to get open

Organization. Same as the V-Cut and Layup drill described on page 44, but this time a defender is introduced. The defensive player positions to see both the player being guarded and the ball. Down in a quick ready position, the defender slides the feet and sticks with the offensive player attempting to cut open for the pass. If the defender denies the pass for 10 sec-

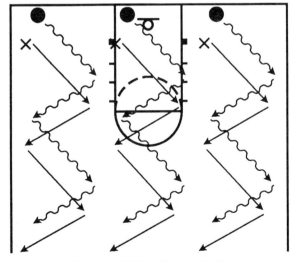

Figure 7.21 Zigzag drill.

onds, the drill is stopped and the offensive player goes to defense.

Coaching Points. Emphasize ball-you-player position to the defender. Encourage offensive players to use this drill to improve their V-, L-, and backdoor cuts.

Name. **Zigzag**

Purpose. To improve footwork when guarding dribblers

Organization. Have players pair up on the baseline, with two pairs in each of three lines. One player in each pair has a basketball and dribbles the length of the court in a zigzag pattern while the partner tries to pressure the dribbler (see Figure 7.21). Have players switch roles when the dribbler reaches the opposite end of the court.

Coaching Points. Have defenders work on their foot movement and staying in the ready position. Warn them not to reach for the ball, but to concentrate on staying with or in front of the dribbler. Tell dribblers not to race downcourt. They should dribble under control, from one side to the other, dribbling with the hand on the side of the direction they are moving.

Rebounding

Rebounding, or gaining possession of a missed shot, is both an offensive and a defensive skill. However, because defensive rebounds (or "boards," as they are called) are especially important for success, the skill is discussed in this defensive skill section.

When a shot is taken, players should not simply stand and watch to see whether it goes in. You must get your players in the habit of positioning themselves advantageously for rebounds. They should react immediately by *boxing out*, getting between the opposing player and the basket and putting the rear in contact with the opponent's body (see Figure 7.22). Tell them to keep their feet active, knees bent with legs ready to spring, and arms and hands up in anticipation of reaching for the ball.

You must warn your players to avoid reaching over an opponent when they get boxed out. They'll get called for a foul if they do. Emphasize the importance of jumping straight up for the rebound. Not only will a vertical jump achieve greater height, but players will stay away from needless fouls if they go straight up.

Figure 7.22   Boxing out.

Here are some additional rebounding tips you'll want to share with your players:

- A shot taken from the side is very likely to rebound to the opposite side of the basket. Therefore, players should try to get *weak side* position when such a shot is taken.
- Pivots are effective maneuvers for gaining inside rebounding position and boxing out. Tell players to simply turn their bodies in front of their opponents and open up to the basket.
- After controlling a rebound, a player should keep the ball close to the body, gripped tightly with both hands in the chest area (see Figure 7.23).

Rebounding Drill

Name. **Glass Cleaner**

Purpose. To improve players' rebounding skill

Organization. Six players at each end of the court. Two lines of three players on each side of the basket, with the first player in each line facing away from the basket, in defensive position against the second player in the line. Coach takes a shot from the free throw line, and defenders try to box out offensive players and get the rebound. When the rebound is secured, the rebounder pivots toward the wing

area on that side of the court and throws a strong overhead pass to the third player in line, who then passes to the coach and takes the offensive position on that side of the court. The original offensive players assume defensive positions, and the rebounders move out to the wing areas to receive the outlet pass from the next rebounder.

Coaching Points. Watch to be sure that players are using good pivots to establish position for the rebound and that they are making some contact with the offensive player to make certain of the player's position. Also, encourage players to be ready and hustle for the ball after it hits the rim. Finally, monitor players' outlet passes for speed and accuracy.

Variation. Glass Cleaner II. This drill is the same as above, except that it incorporates passing by the offense. The coach can pass to either wing player if the defender is not guarding close. And wing players are allowed to shoot (but not dribble) after catching the ball.

Figure 7.23   Proper position after rebound.

How Do I Use Basketball Drills Effectively?

Now you know how to teach the basic individual skills of basketball, but you're probably wondering what drills to use to develop these skills in your players. Before jumping right into the drills, you should consider how you are going to set up your practice sessions to make such activities productive and efficient.

Throughout this unit, basketball drills have been outlined for each skill. When organizing your team for drills, maximize your use of court space to keep as many players active as possible. If you have 12 players on your team and four baskets, try to divide up into groups of 3 for many of your drills. And rather than having 5-on-5 scrimmages with 2 players sitting out, perhaps you can have two games of 3-on-3 going on simultaneously. Or, another option is to have 4-on-4 scrimmages, with the team that's sitting out practicing its offensive plays off to the side.

Here are some more tips for using basketball drills in practices:

- Check that all players on the team know what the drill entails and what is expected of them, before letting them begin.
- Use individual and 2-player drills frequently. These types of drills give each player more "hands-on" practice, and keep all of them more active, than do group drills.
- Use group drills only when the practice facility limits your alternatives (e.g., when there are only two baskets for a shooting drill); to practice teamwork; or to slow down the pace.
- Make sure players have ample space on the court. Assign players to particular baskets, sections of the court, rows, or any other type of arrangement that is best for the drill. Then see to it that they keep in their assigned spots.
- Emphasize performance, not winning, when your players compete in drills. And be sure to match up players by skill and physical maturity to avoid lopsided competition.

How Do I Get My Players to Play as a Team?

To participate in games successfully, kids must not only develop the individual skills presented in unit 7 but also understand and be able to execute team tactics. Therefore, in addition to the basic individual skills, you must teach your players the offensive and defensive team principles of basketball.

What About Team Offense?

In basketball, the offensive team's primary objective is to move the ball effectively and score. A secondary goal is to maintain ball possession so the opposing team cannot score. The following tactics will help your team accomplish these goals.

Offensive Team Principles

Purposeful and efficient movement is essential to the success of a basketball team's offense. Young players, however, have a strong tendency to stand, watch the ball, and holler for the ballhandler to pass the ball to them. Because no one is open or moving to get open, the ballhandler—out of desperation—either puts up a low-percentage shot or tries to force a pass to a teammate. In either case, it's an unsuccessful possession, and the opposing team gets the ball.

Error Detection and Correction for Team Offensive Motion

Offensive players are easy to guard if they just stand in one place. So when you see your team standing around, direct them to move—and move effectively!

ERROR	CORRECTION

Players all standing on one side of the court around the ballhandler shouting for the player to pass them the ball

Figure 8.1 Motion offense.

1. Players should spread out on the court (two of the players without the ball on one side, the other two on the opposite side). Tell the players playing the #2 and #3 positions on offense and those playing the #4 and #5 positions to never stay on the same side of the court for more than 3 seconds.

2. Players should remain active, trying to get open or helping a teammate to get open (see Figure 8.1).

3. If the ballhandler has picked up the dribble, movements to get open must be even quicker and to a position where the player can deliver the ball.

Encourage your players to continually move on offense. But see to it that they move with a purpose. In addition to advising them generally to move away from defenders and to the ball to receive passes, instruct them to do these three things:

- Balance the court.
- Penetrate the defense when possible.
- Set solid screens.

Court Balance

A stationary player is easy to defend; so is an offensive team that is bunched together on the floor. That's why you'll want to teach and remind your players to spread out evenly on their offensive end of the court. When players are arranged in this manner, the path to the basket is less cluttered, and therefore the defense is more susceptible to attack.

Penetration

One of the best ways for an offense to put pressure on the defense is to move the ball into the lane with the pass or dribble. Dribble penetration is effective when the ballhandler keeps the head up and maintains control of the ball. The dribbler can either shoot the ball or pass it to a teammate whose defender has left to stop the

penetrator. Passes are a quicker means of penetration than is the dribble.

Caution players to attempt to penetrate the defense only when the opportunity is present; if they force the ball into the teeth of the defense, they'll likely get called for charging or have the ball stolen. But encourage your players to always look to advance the ball toward the hoop. And be supportive of their attempts to take advantage of openings in the defense, even when they are unsuccessful.

Screens

Because young players often have difficulty getting open to receive or shoot the ball, you should teach them how to set screens for one another. An offensive player who sets a screen, or *pick*, positions himself or herself as a stationary barrier on a side of a teammate's defender; the idea is that the defender's path will be blocked as the teammate cuts around the screen to get open. The screening player stands erect with feet planted shoulder-width apart, keeping the arms down to the sides, and clenching the hands in front of the body below the waist.

Remind players that it does no good to set a screen for a ballhandler who has stopped dribbling. Direct them to "screen away" from

Error Detection and Correction for Screening

Kids have trouble setting and using screens. Too often an offensive player is not patient enough to wait to move until a screener has planted both feet. And just as often, the player setting the screen fails to stay in one place so the teammate can use the screen.

ERROR	**CORRECTION**

Setting moving screens

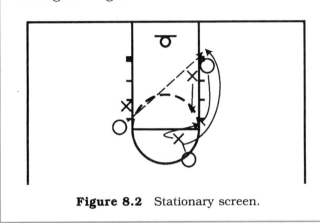

Figure 8.2 Stationary screen.

1. Identify a teammate's defender to set a screen on.

2. Set the screen in a direction that allows the teammate using the screen to go to the basket or to the ball.

3. Plant both feet near the defender, facing the direction opposite to where the teammate will cut.

4. Maintain the position until after the defender makes contact and your teammate has used the screen (see Figure 8.2).

5. Pivot toward the ball.

the ball, meaning they should set screens for teammates who are on the opposite (weak) side of the court from the ball. That way the player for whom the screen is set will be moving toward the passer after coming off the screen. Also, even the best-set screens are worthless if the screen is not used effectively. So work with your players on setting up their opponents and then cutting right by (actually brushing by) the screeners.

General Team Patterns

Guard, forward, and center positions and their responsibilities were described in unit 6. Now let's look at how these players function within an offensive set. (For a diagram of the positions, #1 through #5, see Figure 6.2 on page 35).

The #1 player must bring the ball up the court and initiate the offense. If the offense stalls in the hands of another player, the #1 player should go get the ball and start the offense again. Team organization, penetration, and defensive protection against fast breaks are among the primary concerns of the #1 position.

The #2 and #3 players should assist the #1 player with ballhandling duties when necessary. However, their primary concern should

be to get open to receive a pass on the wings, preferably below the free throw line. Therefore, the #2 and #3 players should move constantly, using screens set by the #4 and #5 players, V-cutting, L-cutting, and cutting backdoor when defenders overplay.

The #4 and #5 players should remain in the lane area, in either the low-post (blocks) or high-post (free throw line) position. These players should constantly help each other get open by setting good, solid screens away from the ball. They should look to set screens for the #1, #2, and #3 players, then pivot and move to the basket looking for a pass and layup. Although the #4 and #5 players must always be concerned about getting a 3-second violation, they should look to get open near the basket on the ball side of the court; and, when on the weak side, they should try to get in good rebounding position.

No matter what type of offense your team runs, these general instructions will help your players understand their roles on the team and their positions on the court. If you fail to effectively inform them, you'll find all five players grouped out near the top of the key, standing around or getting in each other's way. Figure 8.3 illustrates the areas of the court in which the players should run the offensive patterns just described.

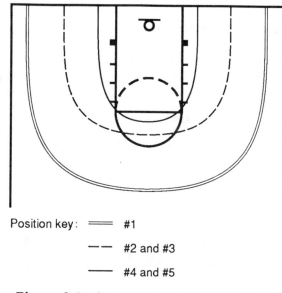

Position key: ═══ #1

‒ ‒ #2 and #3

─── #4 and #5

Figure 8.3 Court areas for player positions.

Teamwork and Shot Selection

Even if your players do a great job of fulfilling their roles on offense, their efforts will all be for naught if they don't work together and shoot high-percentage shots. Although one player on the court makes up only 20% of the team, a lone ''ballhog'' or ''gunner'' can completely destroy the whole offense.

Therefore, in practice make sure that everyone is involved in the offense and that players take the types of shots they should take during games. Remind your players to be patient, that they don't need to take the first 20-footer available. Conversely, several good, crisp passes and solid screens should give your team a good chance to score on every possession.

Special Situations

Inbounds, jump ball, free throws, and fast breaks are some of the special situations your team will need to be prepared for. Don't spend too much time on these aspects of the game, but make certain that your players understand the rules and their duties when such situations arise.

Inbounds. Because youth leagues rarely allow pressing except for the last few minutes of the game, you need not devote practice time to inbounding the ball in the backcourt. Most of your inbound plays should be designed to create an easy scoring opportunity when your team puts the ball into play from underneath

your basket. Keep the plays simple and few. Also, it helps to align in the same manner for each play, both so your players are not confused about where to position themselves and so the defense is not tipped off by a change in formation.

Two options for offensive inbounds are shown in Figure 8.4. But you can use your self-designed plays or those that you have learned from other coaches. The key is to have a good passer inbound the ball and look away from where the play is to go, and for the rest of the team to move quickly to their designated spots.

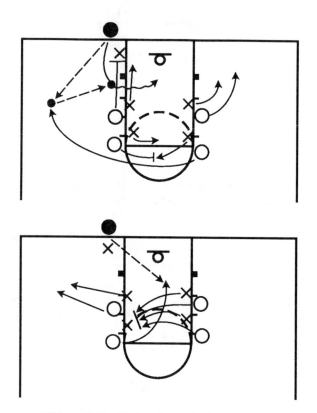

Figure 8.4 Two inbound play options.

Jump Balls. The jump ball procedure was described in unit 6. However, you'll need to give your team some specific guidelines for positioning themselves during games. How players are positioned should depend on whether your team or the opposing team has the better chance of controlling the tip. If the player jumping for you has an advantage, your team should align in an offensive formation and attempt to score off a play (see Figure 8.5a). But if it appears that the opposing team will gain possession a defensive setup is appropriate (see Figure 8.5b).

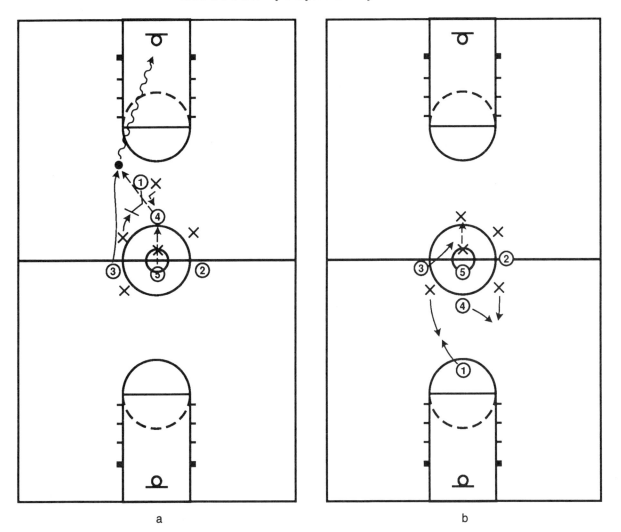

a   b

Figure 8.5 Jump ball formation for (a) offensive and (b) defensive tips.

Free Throws. Much could be said about the proper alignment for free throws. However, the main things you need to remember are these:

- Have your best rebounders in the positions closest to the hoop.
- Remind players to block out the players next to them when the opposing team is shooting.
- Warn players about going over-the-back when the opponent has inside position.
- Designate a player to box out the shooter when the opposing team is shooting.
- Make certain one player is back near midcourt when your team is shooting, to prevent easy fast breaks by the opposition.

Fast Breaks. If your team rebounds well and steals the ball often, you should teach your players the basics of executing the fast break.

The following is only a brief description of what is a very complex part of the game.

When a missed shot is grabbed, the rebounder must pivot with the ball toward the wing area on that side of the court, or downcourt, and hit the outlet (#1, #2, or #3) player. The player who receives the outlet pass should get the ball to the middle of the court, with either the dribble or a pass to the #1 or #2 player. Once the ball is at midcourt, the player with the ball should seek to penetrate with the dribble or pass; however, the player should not drive all the way to the basket unless a lane is open. The remaining four players on the team should rush down the floor—but under control, so if they receive a pass they will not travel. As they cross midcourt, players should make sure they are not headed into a crowded area. Once again, court balance is an important

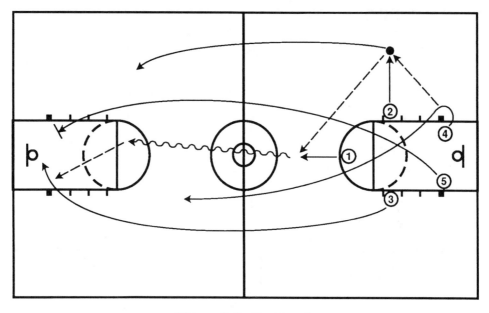

Figure 8.6 Fast break.

Offensive Team Drills

concept to share with your players. An example of the fast break is shown in Figure 8.6.

Name. **3-Player Weave**

Purpose. To help players improve their passing on the move, teamwork, and conversion of lay-up opportunities

Organization. Players are in three lines on one baseline, with the two outside lines just outside of the lane and the middle line centered with the basket. Each player in the middle line has a basketball. The first player in each line begins the drill. The middle player passes the ball to a player in one of the outside lines and runs behind that player. The player who received the pass moves quickly down toward the center of the court, and passes the ball to the player who was in the opposite outside line, and runs behind that player. The player now with the ball makes a pass to the player who began the drill in the middle line and cuts behind that player while continuing to move downcourt. The same sequence continues until players near the opposite basket (see Figure 8.7). At that point, the first player to receive the ball close enough to shoot a layup without dribbling (or traveling) goes strong to the hoop and converts the basket. One player retrieves the ball, and the others move into position and begin the same passing weave to the other end of the court. As the layup is taken at the other end, the next 3-player group begins passing and weaving the other way.

Coaching Points. Players love this drill and the teamwork involved *if* they don't get frustrated learning it. So walk them through it a couple of times to make sure they all get the hang of it. Emphasize quick ball movement and players' making a tight weave as they pass and move down the court. Also stress the importance of scoring after the last pass.

Name. **Moving Triangle**

Purpose. To get players in the habit of maintaining triangle relationships with one another on offense

Organization. At each end of the court there are six players, divided into two teams, and a basketball. Offensive players are required to have at least one foot inside the free throw lane or key area. To avoid crowding and enhance scoring opportunities, the three offensive players spread out in a triangle and alter that formation only momentarily when setting screens for each other. Defenders work on cutting off the passing lane and handling screens set by the offense. The offensive team maintains possession until it commits a turnover or a player leaves the lane or key area.

Coaching Points. Instruct players to keep active but, more importantly, to move with a purpose in mind. Good ballhandling, movement, and team-

lines should be midway between its sideline and its edge of the free throw lane. The third line is at the midpoint of the lane, with one player holding a ball. On the other end of the court, on the free throw line, are two defensive players. The first players in each line run downcourt passing the ball to one another. When the players reach midcourt, the ball goes to the player in the middle. This player must decide how to attack with the 3-on-2 advantage—whether to pass immediately to a teammate or to penetrate with the dribble until a defender intervenes (see Figure 8.8). The defenders can do whatever they wish: Guard the two players in the outside lines, guard the middle player and one outside player, or simply sag off the offensive players and prevent a layup. Whatever they decide, the defenders should get in position to rebound when

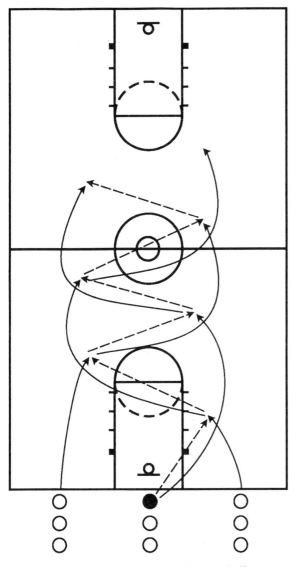

Figure 8.7 3-Player Weave drill.

work should be their primary concerns. As for the defense, remind the defender on the ball to get very close to the ballhandler and get the hands up, and the other two defenders to cut off the passing lane from the players they're guarding.

Variation. Triangle for 2. Same as above, but this time the offense can shoot the ball when a high-percentage shot is available. The offense keeps possession after made shots. Each basket is worth 2 points, with teams playing to 12.

Name. **3-2-1**

Purpose. To practice offensive teamwork when the number of offensive players is greater than the number on defense

Organization. Have players form three lines behind one baseline. Each of the two outside

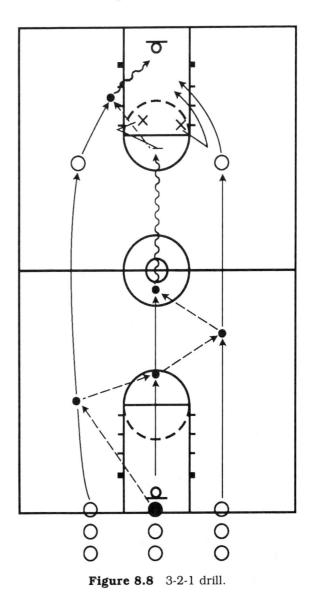

Figure 8.8 3-2-1 drill.

the shot is taken. After the two defenders gain possession, they take the ball to the other end of the court while the player who was originally the middle player on offense attempts to prevent these two from scoring. The players who were originally in the two outside lanes on offense remain on that end of the court while the 2-on-1 situation is played out on the opposite end of the court. These two players then serve as defenders against the next group to come down the court.

Coaching Points. Tell the offensive players, particularly the ballhandler, to make the defenders commit to guarding either the ball or the players away from the ball. In the 3-on-2 situation, have the middle player stop at the free throw line unless the defenders abandon the lane area. Challenge the offense to get nothing but easy, open shots or layups by finding the open player with quick, crisp passes. Let defenders mix up their coverage, but tell them to avoid fouls that might lead to a 3-point play in a game.

What About Team Defense?

Playing good defense involves using correct technique and working together with teammates. Because many youth leagues prohibit zone defenses, and because every player should learn player-to-player defense, this *Rookie Guide* does not describe zone defense principles. The footwork fundamentals and positioning techniques described in unit 7 are essential for *all* players on the team. And, as with offense, if but one player breaks down on defense, the entire defense can collapse.

Defensive Team Principles

Emphasize to your players the proper techniques. And praise them just as much for good defensive play as for scoring. Try to build players' desire to deny their opponents any points and to work as a unit. The following tactics, if performed successfully, will make your team a tough one to score upon:

- Maintain position and balance.
- Cut off the passing lanes.
- Handle screens.
- Help out.

Maintain Position and Balance

Young players often mistakenly attempt to steal the ball by swiping at it with their hands. Advise your players against such steal attempts unless they are certain to get the ball cleanly, because such a defensive maneuver will put them off balance, out of position, and in great jeopardy of being called for a foul. Therefore, encourage your players to play solid defense and refrain from spectacular steal attempts.

Inexperienced players also need help in judging the appropriate distance they should maintain from their offensive opponents. The closer your defenders are to the player with the ball, the more difficult it is for that player to pass and shoot. However, if defenders guard a player too closely—especially a player who has a quickness advantage—they are in danger of getting beat for an easy basket. So tell them to watch their opponent closely during the first few trips downcourt to determine how they match up and which hand the player shoots and dribbles with. And, although this might seem a bit simplistic, advise your players to always be closer to the opponent's basket than are the players they are guarding (for an example, see Figure 8.9).

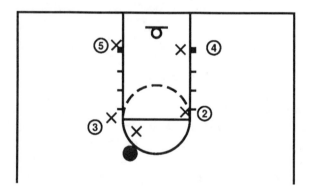

Figure 8.9 Team defense player positions.

Cut Off the Passing Lanes

The best defensive teams make it difficult for the offense to dribble and pass, much less shoot, the ball. Using the player-to-player defensive techniques described in unit 7 and overplaying the opponent's strong hand, your players should be able to force opponents to pick up their dribble. However, preventing passes is sometimes more difficult.

The key to your players' denial of the opposition's passes is to have the four players not guarding the ballhandler maintain ball-you-player position (see Figure 8.10). But this position is an effective deterrent only if defenders are able to watch simultanously the ball and the players they are guarding. And even if players are able to get in position and sight both the players they are guarding and the ball, they still must be quick on their feet to respond to the movements of their opponents.

It's not easy. Kids, and even pros, have

Figure 8.10   Denial defense.

Error Detection and Correction for Defending Off the Ball

Even when they are in good spots to cut off passes to the offensive players they are guarding, kids need to be reminded which way to turn their bodies so they are best able to stick with the players to whom they are assigned.

ERROR

Defenders guarding players away from the ball, facing the ballhandler, or losing track of the player to which they are assigned

Figure 8.11   Defender's position off the ball.

CORRECTION

1. Defenders should be in good position to cut off passes.

2. Every defender should be facing the player to which he or she is assigned (as is the defender in Figure 8.11).

3. From the ready/cut-off position and turned toward the player for whom she or he is responsible, the defender should move the feet quickly in whatever direction the offensive player cuts.

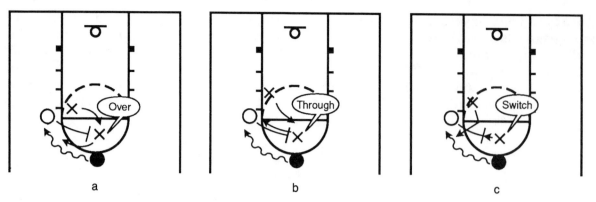

Figure 8.12   Defensive screens: (a) over-the-top, (b) fight through, and (c) switch.

difficulty cutting off the passing lanes. So teach your players this defensive tactic, but be patient with their inability to grasp and execute it.

Handle Screens

Just as you will instruct your players to set screens to get open, so too will the opposing coach. Therefore, your players need to know how to handle screens.

First of all, defenders must learn to communicate with each other. They should be talking throughout each opponent's possession, shouting things like "Look out on the right, Pat!" "I've got weak side!" "Take the ball, Terry!" And, when one of your players sees an opponent setting a screen on a teammate, he or she should immediately holler "Screen right!" or "Screen left!" and the name of the teammate being picked.

Figure 8.12 illustrates the three ways defenders can handle screens. The over-the-top approach should be used when the opponent who uses the screen leaves room for the defender to get around the screener. The defender on whom the screen was set should let the teammate know to stay with the screener, by shouting "Over!" On the other hand, the player being screened should "fight" through it if the teammate whose player is setting the screen leaves room behind the screen and if either defender shouts "Through!" Finally, the defenders should switch the players they are covering when the screener has done an effective job and there is no way that the defender who was screened can stay with the player who used the screen. In this case, the defender whose opponent set the screen should yell "Switch!"

Help Out

No matter how well your players position themselves and communicate on defense, an offensive player will at times spring free. Therefore, you must instruct your players how to respond in these "help" situations.

Your instructions will vary depending on the type of help needed. For example, if one of your players spots an opponent wide open under the basket, waving for a teammate to pass the ball, that defender should leave an assigned opponent who is farther from the basket and sprint to try to prevent the pass. On the other hand, if a dribbler gets by a defender and is headed for a layup, the defensive player closest to the dribbler and between the dribbler and the basket should immediately move in to cut off the lane to the hoop (see Figure 8.13). Whatever the case, the defender who has been beaten, or who loses an offensive player and sees that recovery is impossible, should shout "Help!" All four teammates should be ready

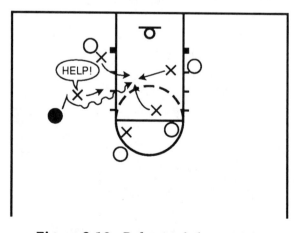

Figure 8.13   Defensive help position.

to respond *if* you have effectively taught them this very important defensive tactic.

Defensive Team Drills

Name. **Screen Solution**

Purpose. To improve defenders' ability to react to screens

Organization. 3-on-3 at each end of the floor, one ball at each end. Offensive players screen for the dribbler and away from the ball in no set pattern. Defenders call out and react to each screen to prevent the offense from scoring. Teams alternate from offense to defense after each possession.

Coaching Points. Emphasize communication and handling screens on defense. See that offensive players set solid, stationary screens and that the teammate for whom the screen was set uses the screen effectively.

Name. **Weak-Side Help**

Purpose. To practice defensive help reactions when a teammate gets beat by an offensive player

Organization. 3-on-3 on each half court, with a coach at each end with a whistle. On every possession, the coach picks a moment to blow the whistle when an offensive player has the ball and is facing the basket. When the whistle is blown, the defender on that player allows the player to drive around to the basket. The player beaten should holler ''Help!'' and the nearest defender moves over to pick up the dribbler. The other two defenders move quickly to cover the two other offensive players (see Figure 8.14). Defensive players should respond similarly if a teammate is beaten before the whistle is blown.

Coaching Points. This is a great drill for working on all aspects of player-to-player defense, so watch that players maintain good ball-you-basket position and cut off the passing lanes. Emphasize swift response by the defense to the call for help. Because of its dynamic nature, this drill will teach players how to help in a variety of situations.

Name. **Get It 'n Go**

Purpose. To practice defensive team pressure, rebounding, and fast-breaking

Organization. 5-on-5 full court with one ball. This is similar to a full-court scrimmage, but with a heavy emphasis on defensive play, defensive rebounding, and running the break. Defenders must overplay the passing lanes and be ready to help any teammate who gets beat by an offensive player. The #3, #4, and #5 position players should own any missed shot by the opponent. The #1 and #2 players should move quickly to outlet positions as soon as a shot is taken. Teams alternate offense as in an actual game.

Coaching Points. Stress defensive teamwork and hustle. Also see to it that your players make quick transitions from defense to offense and from offense to defense.

What Is a Good Way to Scrimmage?

Full-court scrimmages, with the league-standard number of players per team, are fine—in fact they are essential in preparing players for games—but other practice formats have advantages. Small-sided scrimmage formats, such as 3-on-3 on the half court, provide good learning situations. A small-sided, half-court scrimmage places more ballhandling, movement, and defensive responsibilities on each player than does the typical 5-on-5 set. And players love the quick-paced action and greater involvement of 3-on-3 competitions.

You can also organize different types of mini-games, such as games in which no dribbling is permitted. These activities force players to concentrate on certain skills, such as passing and moving. The No Dribble and 7-Up drills

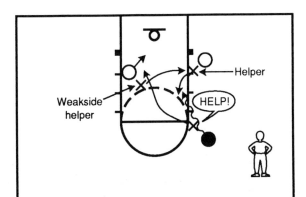

Figure 8.14   Weak-Side Help drill.

described next are just two scrimmage variations that promote participation and teamwork.

Scrimmage Options

Name. **No Dribble**

Purpose. To improve passing and motion skills and get players out of the habit of dribbling needlessly on offense

Organization. Works well 5-on-5, 4-on-4, or 3-on-3 on the half court. The offense is initiated from the top of the key, with the #1 player slapping the ball. The offensive team runs its regular patterns, but the ballhandler is not allowed to dribble (see Figure 8.15). If a player does dribble, the ball is turned over to the defense. If a

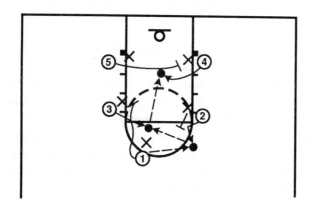

Figure 8.15   No Dribble drill.

team scores, it retains possession. If the defense rebounds a miss, it is allowed a free pass to set up on offense. If the offense rebounds a miss, it can put the ball back up or pass the ball and get back into the offensive motion. Each basket is worth 1 point; the drill is over when one team scores 10.

Coaching Points. Emphasize good passing and motion. Stop play at times if you see improper counterbalance or poor screens being set. Tell players to move the ball quickly, before the defense has a chance to react.

Name. **7-Up**

Purpose. To enhance offensive teamwork and shot selection, and improve team defense

Organization. 5-on-5 full court. The offense must pass the ball at least seven times before shooting, *unless* an uncontested layup opportunity is available. Thus, fast breaks are possible, and the defense can't just take it easy until the sixth pass. Coach blows a whistle after the seventh pass. However, players can continue to pass the ball as much as is necessary to get a good shot.

Coaching Points. Emphasize motion, especially penetration, on offense. Don't let players simply pass the ball seven times out front, far away from the basket. Also, watch that players choose only high-percentage shots—not merely the first thing that comes along after the whistle. Encourage defensive players to maintain good position, talk when screens are set, and help out teammates who get beat.

How Can I Learn More About Coaching and Basketball?

Successful coaches develop only after several years of hard work, learning from their mistakes, and picking up new and effective coaching methods. Indeed, the best coaches continue to seek more information. Here are three ways you can learn more about coaching and basketball.

- *Keep seeking to improve your coaching.* Your players improve when they have fun, are informed, and are motivated to get better. You will too!
- *Attend coaching clinics.* We recommend the Leader Level Course that is offered throughout the country by the American Coaching Effectiveness Program (ACEP).
- *Read up on basketball and coaching.* ACEP offers several basketball coaching resources and an excellent general coaching resource, *Successful Coaching.*

The American Coaching Effectiveness Program would be happy to help you further your coaching knowledge. For information or to order materials, contact us at Box 5076, Champaign, IL 61825-5076 or 1-800-747-5698.

Appendix A

Sample Season Plan for Beginning Basketball Players

Goal: To help players learn and practice the individual skills and team tactics needed to play basketball games successfully.

T = Initial skill teaching time (minutes) ★ = Skills practiced during drills and activities
P = Review and practice time (minutes)

Skills	Week 1		Week 2		Week 3		Week 4	
	Day 1	Day 2	Day 1	Day 2	Day 1	Day 2	Day 1	Day 2
Warm-up	T(10)	P(5)	P(5)	P(5)	P(5)	P(5)	P(5)	P(5)
Cool-down	T(10)	P(5)	P(5)	P(5)	P(5)	P(5)	P(5)	P(5)
Passing								
Chest	T(5)	★		★	★	★	★	★
Bounce	T(5)	★		★	★	★	★	★
Overhead	T(5)	★			★	★	★	★
Drills	P(10)	P(10)	P(10)					
Dribbling								
Stationary		T(5)	★					
Walking		T(5)	★					
Running		T(5)	★	★	★	★	★	★
Drills		P(10)	P(10)					
Shooting								
Layup			T(5)	P(5)	★	★	P(5)	★
Jump			T(10)	P(10)	★	★	P(5)	★
Free throw		T(5)	P(5)	★	P(5)	★	P(5)	★
Drills			P(15)	P(10)	P(10)			
Moving								
Stance			T(5)					
Pivots			T(5)		★	★	★	★
Cuts					T(5)	★	★	★
Drills					P(5)			
Rebounding				T(5)	P(5)	★	★	P(5)
Individual Defense								
Off ball					T(5)	★	★	★
On ball					T(5)	★	★	★
Drills					P(10)	P(5)		

(Cont.)

Skills	Week 1		Week 2		Week 3		Week 4	
	Day 1	Day 2	Day 1	Day 2	Day 1	Day 2	Day 1	Day 2
Offensive Team Play								
Court balance						T(5)	★	★
Motion						T(5)	★	★
Screens						T(5)	P(5)	★
Inbounds							T(5)	P(5)
Fast break							T(5)	P(10)
3-on-3 half-court						P(10)		P(10)
5-on-5 full-court						P(10)		P(10)
Drills							P(10)	
Defensive Team Play								
Position			T(5)		★	★	★	★
Help						T(5)	★	★
Screens						T(5)	★	★
Drills							P(10)	P(10)
Elapsed time	45	50	60	60	60	60	60	60

Appendix B
Official Basketball Signals

Start clock

Stop clock for jump ball

Beckon substitute when ball is dead and clock stopped

Stop clock for foul

Point(s) scored (1 or 2)

Bonus situation (for second throw drop one arm)

Pushing or charging

Illegal use of hand

Technical foul

Holding

Goal counts or is awarded (follow with direction signal)

No score (follow with direction signal)

Traveling (follow with direction signal)

Designates out of bounds spot and direction ball will go

Illegal dribble

3-seconds violation

Over-and-back

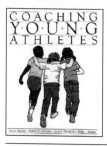

Coaching Young Athletes

Rainer Martens, PhD, et. al.

1981 • Paper • 224 pp
Item BMAR0024
ISBN 0-931250-24-2
$18.00 ($22.50 Canadian)

Coaching Young Athletes introduces and explains the basics of coaching, such as coaching philosophy, sport psychology, sport pedagogy, sport physiology, sports medicine, parent management, and sport law.

It's full of exercises and checklists designed to help you develop a coaching philosophy, improve personal communication skills, understand and use psychological skills, teach skills effectively, prevent, treat, and rehabilitate sport injuries, and understand the legal responsibilities of a coach.

Basketball Skills and Drills

Jerry Krause, PhD

1991 • Paper • 136 pp • Item PKRA0422
ISBN 0-88011-422-3 • $16.95 ($20.95 Canadian)

Master the art of coaching basketball with this new guide by veteran coach Jerry Krause. Over 200 illustrations highlight new drills for ball handling, moving without the ball, shooting, rebounding, defensive play, and more. You'll also learn how to teach offensive and defensive techniques with the help of this reference, whether you are working with young players or high school athletes.

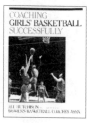

Coaching Girls' Basketball Successfully

Jill Hutchison, EdD, in cooperation with the Women's Basketball Coaches Association

1989 • Paper • 288 pp • Item PHUT0343
ISBN 0-88011-343-X
$20.00 ($25.00 Canadian)

In *Coaching Girls' Basketball Successfully*, you not only learn basketball skills and drills, you also learn how to teach them successfully to your players. This unique text contains

- the building blocks of a successful basketball program,
- over 50 drills and activities,
- 8-week seasonal plans and sample practice plans for three different age levels,
- coaching points and teaching progressions that make learning easier for your players,
- six chapters devoted solely to defensive play and strategy, and
- 180 illustrations showing various drills and proper technique.

Coaching Girls' Basketball Successfully is the ideal text for you to teach basketball basics more successfully to players from the 5th grade through high school.

Prices subject to change

Coaching Basketball Successfully

Morgan Wootten

Foreword by John Wooden

1992 • Paper • 240 pp • Item PWOO0446
ISBN 0-88011-446-0
$18.95 ($23.50 Canadian)

Coach Morgan Wootten has redefined the word *success* in basketball. Whatever level you coach at, you'll appreciate the way he takes sophisticated techniques and breaks them down into practical skills, strategies, and drills that you can apply in your own program. Wootten also explains the importance of developing a coaching philosophy—how success should be measured in terms of effort and execution rather than outcome.

Contents

Developing a Basketball Coaching Philosophy • Communicating Your Approach • Motivating Players • Building a Basketball Program • Planning for the Season • Preparing for Practices • Basic Offensive Positions, Skills, and Sets • Teaching Offensive Skills • Developing a Running Game • Developing a Half-Court Game • Special Situations • Basic Defensive Skills and Strategies • Teaching Defensive Skills • Teaching Team Defense • Preparing for the Game • Handling Game Situations • Evaluating Players • Evaluating Your Program • Motivational Messages • Sample Monthly Practice Plan

Basketball Coaches' Corner Teaching Tape

Women's Basketball Coaches Association

(90-minute videotape)

Item MWBC0025 • 1/2" VHS
$39.00 ($48.50 Canadian)

Treat your team to a private clinic given by four of the most successful women's collegiate basketball coaches. Easy-to-follow demonstrations, practical teaching drills, and insightful commentary on ball handling, dribbling, rebounding, catching, free throws, hook shots, footwork, shooting, passing, and post defense show your players how to master the fundamentals of basketball.

ACEP Volunteer Level

The American Coaching Effectiveness Program (ACEP) now provides two excellent youth coaches' courses: the Rookie Coaches Course and Coaching Young Athletes Course. The Rookie Coaches Course not only introduces coaches to the basic principles of coaching, but also teaches them how to apply those fundamentals as they instruct young athletes in the rules, skills, and strategies of their particular sport. This *Rookie Coaches Basketball Guide* serves as a text for the course.

The second coaching education option at the Volunteer Level is the Coaching Young Athletes Course. This alternative is for coaches who have completed the Rookie Coaches Course successfully and coaches who want to receive more instruction in the principles of coaching than is offered in that course.

ACEP encourages youth sport coaches to complete both the Rookie Coaches and Coaching Young Athletes Courses. We believe the combined learning experiences afforded by these courses will give you the coaching background you need to be the kind of coach kids learn from and enjoy playing for.